c/o Postmaster

c/o Postmaster

Thomas R. St. George

New York • Thomas Y. Crowell Co.

TO PHOEBE

INTRODUCTION

Last January from somewhere in Australia there drifted into the office of the San Francisco *Chronicle* a piece, written with what may best be described as a kind of cockeyed seriousness, describing the life of an American soldier in that curiously new Antipodean world. With the piece were some drawings in which the author-artist's definitely fourth-dimensional approach was, if possible, even more manifest than in his prose. Accompanying the material was a letter, rather on the plaintive side, explaining that this was Number 14 in a series, that the idea was that the *Chronicle* just might like the stuff enough to print it, and that if so the signatory to this document would be pleased and proud. The letter was signed, of course, by Corporal Thomas R. St. George, who added that maybe the other pieces hadn't come through yet, but if the Editor would just wait, they probably would.

Corporal St. George had been long enough in the Army to understand the significance of the phrase, Through Channels. His Number 1 piece is still somewhere In Channels, perhaps stuck there for the duration. But others did come along — Number 11, Number 4, Number 8 and so on, complete with neat rectangles cut by the censor's scissors. And they were all wonderful. Yes, to be sure that's a loose kind of word. But they were, and so were the pictures. The *Chronicle* printed them and the paper's readers loved them.

As for the book, C/O POSTMASTER, the reader will soon discover for himself its peculiar charm.

If you'd like information, of course, there's a lot of it here. St. George doesn't miss much. Here is the young American learning about fish and chips, about tea and scones, discovering that ice cream is an "ice," that liquor is "plonk," that hard candy is "lollies," that there is a perennial shortage of

Coca-Cola and female companionship, that Australian money is confusing, that the way you say "Who do you think you're kidding?" is "Aw, break it down!" and that Koala beer is no beer at all, but a kind of glorified strawberry pop. Those who enjoy enlightenment in such matters will find it in this book, sometimes even pretty seriously expressed. The American soldier is learning from his new Australian friends and they are learning, fast, from him. It's all very global and neighborly, and St. George gets it nicely into his book.

And I should like to put forward another reason for reading C/O POSTMASTER. That reason is to make the acquaintance of Corporal St. George himself, through his text and pictures.

But you'd better make up your own mind about him. One thing, he's a very American guy. You'll find that out before you've read three pages. On second thought, that's by all odds the best reason for reading C/O POSTMASTER.

JOSEPH HENRY JACKSON

Berkeley, California

PREFACE

WE'LL SKIP the explanations, but I'd like to thank: The United States Army for furnishing, perchance unwittingly, several typewriters and most of the paper on which this book was written. The manufacturers of Coca-Cola for providing, and the United States Army Service Forces and the Merchant Marine for getting that product overseas; and said Army Service Forces for a like performance when it came to cigarettes, without which this book could not have been written. The editors of the "This World" section of the San Francisco *Chronicle* for first publishing some of the material. Captain Herbert L. Krueger for his somewhat lenient attitude regarding just what happened to all those things "I forgot" to do while writing. First Lieutenant Ervin J. Sanders for the use of his gas lantern night after night, and Sergeant Eugene Sprecher for some elementary instruction in how to get it started. Sergeant Ray Dasmann who (and the Editors can believe this or not) helped me a great deal with the spelling. Master Sergeant John King who posed (at professional fees) for a good many of the illustrations and suggested as a title: "For chrissake, St. George!"

With most of us this army career is by far the greatest experience we will ever have. I only hope that in reading about a few of these experiences you get half the kick out of it that we got when they were happening to us. Some of the characters are *not* entirely fictitious, but their resemblance to any person, living or dead, is incidental and done without malice aforethought.

C/O Postmaster   R. St. G.
San Francisco, California

CONTENTS

ON SHIPMENT

ONE BRIGHT MORNING, early in the spring of 1942, fifty-seven average young men were routed out of a West Coast barracks at the brutal hour of 5 A.M., pushed into the semblance of a straight line, and informed by a captain (who played to the hilt this reasonable facsimile of a "zero hour") that they were on shipment. At least six of the fifty-seven received this news with practically no feeling whatsoever, having spent the night wallowing in what passed for vice in Paso Robles, California. Particularly one of them, a married man himself, had talked with a waitress for all of ten minutes, or until she'd repeated several times that she was married herself, to a sergeant in Fort Lewis. The others had sat around and gloried in such wallowing, smoked too much, drunk too many alleged whiskey-cokes, and come home by special request of the Provost Marshal.

Now, at 5 A.M., they were in no way as bright as the morn-

1

ing. But such is the power of the G.I. mind that before break-fast was over all were firmly convinced they would arrive at Fort Leonard Wood in time for a week-end pass, and two had laid exhaustive plans as to what they would do first chance they got home to Des Moines. All of which resulted from a chance remark, dropped by a lieutenant colonel and overheard by a K.P., to the effect that men on shipment would be leaving the Ninth Corps Area.

Well, great! We were leaving the Ninth Corps Area! Back to the Middle West. It was with reasonably light hearts that we packed our barracks bags. (Reasonably light hearts and shoes and socks and three kinds of underwear and a carton of cigarettes and a cherished garrison cap and a sheaf of old letters.) Whistled outside for the last time at eight-thirty, we were lined up in a double row and minutely inspected for scuffed shoes and unbuttoned buttons. No commander in his right mind would think of turning a soldier over to an-other commander without said soldier's looking ten degrees snappier than an enlistment poster. Soldiers with flat feet, yes; soldiers with a rifle score of 35, yes; confirmed goldbricks and cigarette moochers, take 'em and you're welcome, sir; but sloppy soldiers, never!

Buttoned to the ears and standing at attention, we listened to a short lecture (prepared by the War Department and butchered by a second lieutenant) to the effect that we were undoubtedly the finest type of Young Americans, leaving to defend our heritage. We thought of the advantages of defend-ing a heritage in Fort Leonard Wood as compared with San Luis Obispo and were considerably happier than our lieu-tenant throughout the performance. Our company com-mander, who had been with us something under two weeks, then bid us good-by and good luck and added that we were potentially the finest soldiers he had *ever* seen. We were deeply impressed.

Staff Sergeant Beerbodt, recently promoted on the strength of our improved appearance after thirteen weeks of his guidance, led us as we straggled across the parade ground. Not once did he shout, "Cover off! Soldier up!" Now it is naturally impossible to march decently with two barracks bags taking turns at knocking the legs from under one and Sergeant Beerbodt knew this as well as we did; but thirteen weeks before, when we were raw recruits, Sergeant Beerbodt had led us across this same parade ground and that night he had barked at us constantly, "Pick it up! Pick it up! Stay in line!" As of then, we hated Sergeant Beerbodt passionately. During thirteen weeks of listening to Sergeant Beerbodt shout, "Right shoulder . . . HARMS! Forward . . . HARCH! C'mon, c'mon, DO it!," our hatred increased until at times it threatened to choke us.

But now, as we straggled across our parade ground for the last time, Sergeant Beerbodt was suddenly a friend. At least his ugly face was familiar and only the night before he had confided to three of us (over a beer that we had purchased, which may have had something to do with it) that we were, "Aw'-right guys only you louse around too much." And he'd given us a bit of advice: "Just keep your nose clean an' don't get caught lousin' around an' you will be okay." We'd learned a lot of things from Sergeant Beerbodt besides the Manual of Arms. So now, as we waited at the edge of the parade ground for nobody knew just what, we offered him a cigarette. And he—it was the first time in our experience—countered with one of his own.

More soldiers arrived as we waited, straggling across the parade ground from all directions, and all, we discovered, quite sure that they were going to Alaska or Los Angeles or Texas or the Portland Air Base. We held ourselves somewhat aloof; obviously we were going to Fort Leonard Wood for a reason. To form the nucleus of a new division, it was decided,

and presently there was a spirited discussion as to how much money a tech sergeant made. We would all be tech sergeants immediately, of course, with a new division.

Eventually there were olive drab overcoats and blue barracks bags scattered along five hundred yards of parade ground. Half a dozen officers remained apart, bearing the weight of the war on their shoulders, while we enlisted men sat around and talked of girls and home and various towns in the vicinity of various camps. Next to me two lawyers discussed at length the divorce laws of the State of Washington. Most of us, I think, in spite of what we had offered at times during the past weeks if only we could "Get outa this HOLE," were really sorry to be going. Leaving a home is always sad, and a soldier has so many homes.

And the Army has an antidote. After two hours spent sitting on a barracks bag (which invariably has a pair of shoes, heels up, directly beneath the back of a guy's lap when he sits down) or the granulated surface of a parade ground, anything, even an Army truck, looks like a change for the better. At long last such trucks arrived, and after a considerable

4

amount of lining up and counting off, we were ordered into them. Those of us who fancied we were going east had somehow imagined we would travel in the comparative comfort of a troop train, but having had nothing to do with planning our itinerary (and because it was an order) we took the trucks.

In fact, we made a concerted rush for them, proving once and for all that we were veterans by everybody's trying to get in first and sit at the back where he could at least see where he'd been if not where he was going. After a certain amount of waiting and the addition, under protest, of three more soldiers complete with barracks bags, we pulled out. Civilian traffic being blocked off, we roared through the Main Gate without slackening speed. We derived a strange pleasure from this. It was the only time any of us had ever come through that gate without showing a pass to the M.P.

An Army truck as a means of transportation may be excellent for shipping cabbage or livestock, but as rubberneck bus it is a fizzle. All I saw as we roared north was the back of the guy's neck that sat on my lap, a peculiarly uninspiring view. And a convoy, when seen from the rear seat of a passing sedan, may look very impressive and may even fill the sedan's occupants with a fleeting pride in the "power and the might of the American Army"; but like a parade, it is best appreciated from the sidelines. The steel-helmeted troops sitting grimly in the backs of the trucks are probably impressed not at all with the "power and the might." They are chiefly interested in finding a speck of what passes for comfort while en route; they wait hopefully while some hardy soul lights a cigarette and promptly bum him for a light; they'd like to know who the hell is trying to sprawl in a truck full of twenty-two men; and they wonder vaguely how long it will be before their driver

6

hooks the corner of a concrete spillway and jars everybody loose from his heredity. That he will hit one sooner or later they know.

Thus we roared north. Three times we stopped so that a lieutenant might stick his head over the endgate and count us. This counting is an important part of all troop movements, there being a not unfounded belief that in any given number of soldiers being moved from one place to another ten per cent will, without even trying, become "lost" unless closely watched and carefully counted. The fact that our truck was accused at various times of containing 23, 19, and 18 men has nothing to do with it. Nor can the fact that on arrival two trucks were discovered missing be considered as proof of anything. Quite possibly somebody forgot to count the trucks. All of which is the kind of thing soldiers mean when they say "the old Army game."

Anyway, we arrived. Exactly where was questionable, but we detrucked in one of those slow, penetrating drizzles California reserves for soldiers who insist they would rather be back home in Sioux City. We attempted to reclaim our barracks bags as they were hurled out of the trucks by soldiers doing their best to resemble old and calloused baggage handlers. Then we waited. Various non-coms wandered about wondering audibly as to who we were and where did we belong? One of us who fancied himself a man of the world asked a corporal, "How long yu been in, Pal?"

"Twenty-two months," the corporal told him.

We subsided. These men were veterans.

Eventually an officer arrived and herded us into a barracks. He was visibly worried to find that we had arrived with nothing in the way of equipment outside of gas masks and went off muttering that we were supposed to arrive with everything *except* gas masks. He was replaced, presently, by a first lieutenant, who herded us into a mess hall, and, when we were

7

done eating, led us back to the barracks, told us to stay there. His duty done, he promptly disappeared. He, in turn, was replaced by a first sergeant who informed us we were temporarily assigned to "Hache" Co. ("It says 'G' on the buildings, but it's Hache!"), and mustn't go away because somebody might want us. He seemed extremely doubtful as to whether or not anybody would actually want us, and was on the point of disappearing himself but stopped at the door, and in the manner of a great man dispensing small favors told us, "You can take them ties off now. We don't wear 'em here."

Religiously we removed our ties. And gathered in little groups the forty-one of us who were left (the remaining sixteen, as far as I know, are still roaring north in the back of an Army truck and should be well along on the Alaskan Highway by this time) decided—not without misgiving—that "we just came in out of the rain."

As it turned out, this idea was somewhat erroneous. The next time any of us mentioned it we were six hundred miles off the coast of Hawaii. By that time we had become more or less resigned to the series of jolts that transformed us, in something less than a week, from the Basic Training or "Glorified Boy Scout" stage of soldiering to the ranks of rough, tough, case-hardened, blasé Combat Troops en route to a Theater of Operations. In a word: no, we did not go to Fort Leonard Wood.

Considerable doubt as to the exact whereabouts of our destination crept in while we were still temporarily assigned to "Hache" Co. By dint of persistent questioning we discovered that "Sure, this outfit has trucks, but they's all at the Point of Embarkation!" We learned too that the remainder of the company or "old men" were entirely National Guardsmen or low-numbered selectees with eighteen months of service including the Louisiana Maneuvers behind them. We "new men," who still figured our service in weeks, felt out of our depth. Then, late the second afternoon, we were herded into the supply room and issued new "coal scuttle" helmets. These, while undeniably a safer hat than our former "Dache" models, were still scarce enough in the spring of '42 to make us wonder just why *we* should be so honored. Unless, of course, we were . . . But no! They couldn't send *us!* We weren't *ready!*

Ready or not we spent the following A.M. listening to a lecture on "Shipboard Discipline" and some off-the-record but highly colorful accounts of the Louisiana Maneuvers as seen by an enlisted man who began them as a sergeant and finished them digging latrines. In the afternoon we "new men" were given a physical examination and an interview.

The former consisted of perfunctory tappings and the question: "Is there anything wrong with you?" The accepted answer being (except in the case of a young man who had lost part of his plate in transit and was therefore quite helpless when confronted with G.I. food) "No, Sir." The interview too, like a Post Exchange haircut, was short and quick. "What did you do in civilian life?" they asked us; "Next man!" Did the interviewing officer suspect a gleam of intelligence or discover a potential company barber, he took the man's name.

Immediately following our physical and interview we were permanently assigned in alphabetical order, which might lead one to believe that our various abilities were not too carefully weighed. But, as one company commander explained to a bunch of the boys who showed up in a rifle platoon protesting that they were "communications men," what the Army really wanted was qualified killers, one to a gun. This little speech went a long way toward reviving the battered spirits of the misplaced communications men. It restored to them the feeling that they were important and led them to appear noticeably murderous for several weeks. Eleven of us, from Reem, Robert, to Terrell, Opaz, plus a strange youth who arrived via typographical error and was questioned at length concerning how the hell you pronounced "R-f-f-e-l-d-t," found ourselves intact and assigned to a headquarters company. Where we listened to a short succinct speech by the C.O., the gist of which was: "You men are going on a trip, by boat, and what you don't need, get rid of!" Ready or not we were going.

Generally speaking there was a mad rush to write, wire, and phone home, collect. And there were sundry blanks to fill in and forms to fill out, including a postcard signed by us and addressed to our "Next of Kin" but mailed (we sincerely hoped) sometime in the future by an official source, that conveyed the most banal but welcome message I ever hope to send anybody: "Arrived safely at destination." Incidentally, the words "next of kin" appeared on all these blanks with what seemed to me a thoroughly discouraging and unnecessary prominence.

Then there was a considerable amount of packing and repacking to be done. That which we thought we would need or could use while aboard ship we put in a barracks bag marked "*A* bag"; said bag to be our constant companion for the duration of the voyage. That which we decided we could neither need nor use until after "arriving safely at destination" we put in a "*B* bag," this one to travel on its own with no guarantee that we would ever see it again. On finishing my first packing I found this *B* bag contained one tool, entrenching. Two strong men could scarcely lift my *A* bag. On the off chance that we would "arrive safely" in Australia, which was reputedly hot and dry, I added overshoes and two blankets and some odd garments affectionately known as "longjohns" to the *B* bag (had we "arrived safely" in Alaska I would have suffered horribly) and eventually, after re-

peated efforts and a brutal slashing of nonessential goods, I got my *A* bag down to a mere eighty pounds.

Finally there was one last pass. Four of us took it together, spending a rather delightful Sunday afternoon—our "last in the good old U.S.A.," as we frequently reminded each other —in Monterey, a town that we had never seen before, will probably never see again, and did not see very much of that afternoon. Having a total of something like two dollars (borrowed) myself, I thought the prevailing spirit of "one for all and all for one" suited me admirably. And the fact that we were possessed of vital strategic knowledge—knowledge of supreme importance to the war effort—not to be bandied lightly about with the casual young lady acquaintances who became attached to us for rations and quarters in one of the bars, but only hinted at—more broadly as the day wore on—added greatly to our enjoyment. Frankly, the young ladies were impressed not at all with our guarded remarks concerning this imminent departure to fight, as one of us put it, "For *their* homes and *their* unborn children." Probably they'd heard substantially the same story from innumerable Presidio inductees on their way to Camp Haan.

Somewhat later, when not one of us could dance and two of us showed signs of becoming violently ill, the young ladies left. We took a taxi back to camp. At least we'd gone out in the approved fashion.

So long town.

THE FOLLOWING DAY had all the aspects of a knock-down bargain sale. At noon we were "alerted." This corresponds to the yellow light on a traffic signal and meant that theoretically we were ready to move on an hour's notice. It meant also that the soldiers who had taken their last pass on Monday (because Sunday was a day off anyway) must be rounded up and returned to camp, but quick. M.P.'s were dispatched in anything that would roll to scour the surrounding countryside and drag these soldiers home. Some very disgusted and heartbroken soldiers they dragged home, too. One in particular, an acquaintance of ours, was forcibly separated from a young lady just as they were on the point of leaving for an intimate little picnic. He has never quite recovered.

Along about three some quartermaster trucks arrived full of equipment and laundry. The laundry had been washed but was still wet and no attempt had been made to separate it. The equipment, too, had evidently been loaded at something less than a moment's notice, being a hopeless jumble of tents, shoes, chinos, mess kits, packs, and overshoes. To sign and receive for such a mess would have been impossible, and the supply sergeant (whose nerves were pretty well shot by that time anyway) threatened to go berserk were it even suggested. So rather than try it they scattered everything around the supply room, invited the company to file through and "Take whatcha want, but remember, you gotta carry it." The new men were forbidden to try on any laundry because they hadn't sent any. That was the sole concession to ethics.

This little game was still going full blast when more trucks arrived and hauled away our *B* bags. Then word came down that WE would move out at six sharp. I was in the supply room at the time, searching for the other half of a pair of 10-EE shoes, which isn't my size but was still a hell of a lot better than bare feet. On hearing the news about our departure I felt nothing in particular except a deeper urge to find that other shoe. I think it affected our first sergeant the same way. He was with me in the supply room at the time, feverishly trying on freshly laundered field jackets. Being a large man, he was having some difficulty in finding one that fit until—just as somebody stuck his head in the door and yelled, "We fall out at six o'clock!"—he came up with a size 48. Ignoring the interruption, he zipped it on and squealed (as much like a little child as a first sergeant can squeal), "Now I got TWO field jackets!" Presently I found another shoe and dashed off to cram it into my *A* bag.

Back in the barracks something of significance had appeared on the bulletin board. "Tomorrow's K.P.'s" had been gleefully crossed out, and added at the bottom of the roster, in scrawling print, was the information: "NEW ADDRESS —C/O POSTMASTER, SAN FRANCISCO."

That did it. "C/O Postmaster." I was going overseas, away
from home, to God knew where or what or for how long,
maybe the rest of my life. And there was too much to do to
give a particular damn about the significance of it all. Probably it was just as well.

Now when my Uncle Harry went overseas with the first
A.E.F. he marched down Atlantic Avenue at high noon and
it was quite an occasion. Whistles blew. Everybody and his
brother turned out to cheer or wave a flag. The regimental
band played "Good-by Broadway, Hello France." As Uncle

Harry told it, there were even some girls around to kiss the boys good-by. (Uncle Harry did not exactly go overseas, but was sent to Norfolk, Virginia, where he remained until January, 1919. But he was heart, soul, and stomach for the American Legion and seldom mentioned Norfolk.) Anyway, as Uncle Harry put it, when he left Boston he was "psychologically ready" to go overseas.

Psychologically I wasn't worth a damn when we detrained at Frisco. Of all the things I would rather not do, stumbling through a blacked-out freight yard at one A.M. with my arms full of barracks bag and a rifle belting me across the back of

the neck at every third step is the one thing I would rather not do the most. Nor were there any girls around. Practically speaking we could have taken the ferry to Oakland and nobody the wiser. At the entrance to the pier were slouched a couple of shifty-eyed characters who looked as if they had been plucked bodily out of a "Don't Talk! The Enemy Listens!" poster. Inside were some longshoremen who didn't deign to interrupt a blackjack game for our departure, and assorted M.P.'s who stood around muttering, "Put them cigarettes out." The regimental band played nothing, their repertoire being limited to one of the members hitting the man in front of him on the helmet at regular intervals with a long piece of pipe that serves as a gas alarm, and the man who was hit snarling, "For chrissake, watch what you're doin' with that goddamn thing!" A few of us hummed "Good-by Mama, I'm Off to Yokohama," but it was far from the spirited singing usually associated with the fade-out of a Hollywood Marine epic.

The actual loading went off smoothly enough. In alphabetical order (naturally) we shuffled toward the gangplank. As each man reached the shore end, a steamship official, assisted by a colonel, referred to a long list of names and read the man's surname. Did the man answer with his correct first name and middle initial they thumbed him up the gangplank. Beyond a momentary but maddening desire to tell them mine was "Hosaki, Nitzu" and go blithely on my way up Market Street, I got aboard without any undue excitement. And that is how we went off to war in 1942. Strictly a business proposition.

Once aboard we were rapidly assigned to cabins. Knowing little or nothing about boats except that usually, when sunk, the top went down last, I was relatively happy to find myself, along with 165 others, on "A" deck, in what had formerly been the Gentlemen's Smoking Salon, but was referred to by the steward (a nervy chap) as "our stateroom." Incidentally, this steward, before he left us, completely ruined what remained of my first night's sleep by remarking that "A" deck, though cooler, would probably be cut to bits with disgusting regularity by strafing fire in the form of .50-caliber machine-gun slugs. He went on to describe, in detail, the lack of protective armor over our heads, then suggested that I, being thin, should take a top bunk. Where I slept on my side and dreamed that I was neatly centered in a gun sight.

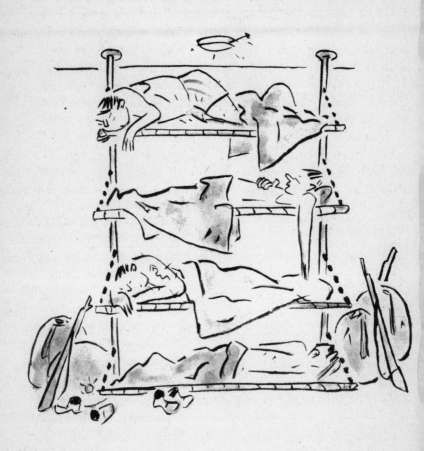

ON WAKING the next morning I was somewhat reassured to find that so far at least there were no bullet holes in the roof. And on going outside, fully prepared to see what is generally described as "an endless expanse of heaving green water," I found that we were at most two feet from land in the form of the same pier. I had, it seemed, another day to live.

Which I spent until almost noon standing in an endless mess line that wound down, down, down into the bowels of the ship, arriving finally (along about 11 A.M.) in what had been the Dining Salon but was now the Troops Mess. In the afternoon several of us attempted to wander farther through the ship but kept running into signs that said "Troops Not Allowed" and sailors matching quarters. We watched other sailors, quite blue in the face from their efforts to appear nonchalant, strip the ship's guns for action and listened to some harrowing if sketchy accounts of past actions in which these very guns had played a prominent part. Two soldiers who had enlisted from San Francisco spent the entire day hanging over the rail, staring at The Mark, trying to pick out the houses of girls they had known, and reminiscing generally. From three to five we stood in line for another meal.

As I was coming up from this chow I met a young man who looked as if he had suddenly and without premeditation swallowed a live frog. "We're MOVING!" he gasped. "Yu

gotta put cha life belt on!" On deck were innumerable other young men, all of whom looked as if they too had swallowed frogs. It was true. We were moving.

Out into the bay, past Alcatraz, the plight of whose occupants we favorably and profanely compared with our own. I heard six men offering to trade shoes and serial numbers sight unseen with any of the occupants including A. Capone. Past the Presidio, which induced some very ribald remarks about "garrison soldiers" in general and Presidio garrison soldiers in particular. Past Fisherman's Wharf. Through the Golden Gate, after a brief but hopeless discussion about maybe our smokestack wouldn't clear the bridge. It did. Past Land's End.

From the superstructure on down there were soldiers, hanging any place there was room to hang, most of them cracking wise whether they felt like it or not. Some very bad tenors (disguised as second lieutenants) rendered (to bits) an unpurged version of "Christopher Columbo." Two guys who thought they saw a girl on the bridge fought over a pair of field glasses. It would add a nice touch had I seen some granite-jawed colonel wiping a tear off his nose, but the only colonel I saw, saw me at the same time and roared, "You there! Get the hell away from that gun mount!"

For most of us it was the first and possibly the last time we would ever see the Golden Gate. Suddenly, it struck me as a spot that has never been done justice in the newsreels. Never, in fifteen minutes, have I become so attached to anything as that bridge. The only view that can ever beat it will be the same view, coming the other way. But that night, suddenly, it was gone. And I felt suddenly, utterly, and completely alone; this in spite of six soldiers who were leaning and hanging on the back of my neck.

Somewhat later half a dozen of us gathered in a cabin that we were to know intimately as the days went by. For soldiers we were very quiet. We figured we were outside the three-mile limit, the Continental Limits of the United States, and that so far our twenty-per-cent extra pay for Overseas Service had amounted to something like two cents. We knew we were eligible to join and become bona fide members of the American Legion and discussed, without much enthusiasm, the possibilities of future conventions. But the specter of the Golden Gate fading into the east hung over us like the spirit of stingy Uncle John at the reading of his will. We broke it up and went to bed.

Except two of us who ventured a few brief moments on the promenade deck. It was a very black night. There was a considerable amount of wind, at least a gale, we thought. The ship creaked and groaned and was evidently on the point of breaking in half. The water appeared horribly deep, it was certainly heaving, and in all probability it was quite green. So was my face (green) and my stomach (heaving).

THE TRIP ACROSS was uneventful. The excitement of being afloat and the possible objective of one of Tojo's pig boats lasted about a week. From there on in it was just monotonous. And the lovers of the sea can say what they want to about its "ever changing aspects": it always looked the same to me. Blue in the daytime, black at night, never a gas station nor a drive-in stand nor a sign that said "Cabins $1.00." Personally, I'll do my traveling on Highway 101.

For a time we sailed under the soft white light of a romantic tropic moon, as plugged by Cook Tours, but even that failed to impress me. A tropic moon is certainly bigger than our middle-western variety, and its light is soft enough and white enough, but there is too damn much of it. Throughout the voyage I favored dark windy nights with a thick fog; such nights, according to the crew, being very bad for pig boats.

Anyway, this trip was no Cook Tour. The romantic possibilities of a troopship are practically worthless. True, it was rumored there were some real live "Nurses!" aboard one of the ships in our convoy, and several soldiers strained their eyes to a degree and burnt hell out of the bridges of their noses in an effort to discover which ship it was. On the slim chance, I guess, that we would be sunk and set adrift on a life raft, as portrayed by *Esquire* cartoons. Well, we never were. And beyond exclaiming two or three times a day, "SEE!

There in the white! That's a nurse! Boy, how'd you like to be on *that* ship!" these Lotharios had little better time than the rest of us.

And the rest of us did not even look romantic. Living as we did, mostly in a life belt and a filthy pair of chinos, the one thing we needed most was a strong blast of Chanel No. 5. The whole ship smelled like a very small dressing room at the height of the football season, or Coney Island with an offshore wind. But that had its compensations. Such as you will never know until you have lived in a stateroom (double) with eight other guys and no ventilation to speak of, but plenty of magazines full of ads lamenting the utter social desolation of a young man completely bereft of his friends because he forgot to use Mum.

As we entered the tropics what little romance may still have clung to us gave up the unequal struggle. Ronald Colman may look romantic in a dirty shirt and a stubble of beard, but we certainly didn't. It was here that the cueball haircut—later known as the "Guinea clip"—became quite popular. The amateur barbers (any guy with a shears and some self-confidence) did a rushing business, even the boys with the naturally curly deciding that perhaps they could do with a little less insulation. There is no denying that a guy with a cueball haircut resembles, to a marked degree, a badly sheared sheep, but that is what he pays for—comfort, not

style. I held onto my self-respect by the scant margin of a half inch, but I know it was a horrible disappointment to the sadist who wielded the clippers.

But outside of the shaving (daily, as prescribed by regulations, be the water salt, fresh, or bilge) and the general Coney Island atmosphere (which made some of us sick and the New Yorkers homesick), the trip was what is usually described as "the life of Riley." Eating and sleeping, always of great interest to soldiers, were to be had in quantity. Mess was served three times daily, theoretically by decks, but there was nothing to prevent a hungry and dishonest soldier from eating with two or even three decks. The chow, as a rule, was very good after the first four days. (It may have been just as good the first four days too, but it didn't *look* as good.)

Breakfast invariably produced two hard-boiled eggs. Personally that didn't bother me. I like eggs. Still, morning after morning, two hard-boiled eggs . . . It wasn't long before the wittier spirits began cackling and crowing as they were presented with their morning eggs. As the days went by (and it was easy to tell how many days had gone by; we divided by two the number of hard-boiled eggs we had eaten) more and more soldiers took to greeting their breakfast with a cluck-cluck. It got to the point where the K.P.'s, who must have handled something like 84,000 eggs during the course of the voyage and listened to at least half that many imitations of a hen, wanted to jump overboard. They were forcibly prevented.

Possibly these eggs doubled as ballast. Anyway, there were still a considerable number of them left when we "arrived safely at destination" and certain unscrupulous soldiers who remained on board to help with the unloading, unloaded the eggs on the populace, bootlegging them through the streets of the port of debarkation as "absolutely fresh eggs, right off the boat." The natives, having suffered a prolonged egg shortage, went for this little story hook, line, and pound note, to the tune of a neat profit for said unscrupulous soldiers and another blow to International Friendship when they got the eggs home and tried to make omelets. Hard-boiled eggs don't omelet.

When it came to sleeping we had a choice of two places: inside, where, in my case at least, having the top bunk in a tier of four, there seemed a reasonable chance that not too many people would step on my face; or outside, where it was considerably cooler, but somewhat crowded and more than a little bit public. The chief disadvantage being a group of inveterate crap shooters who slaved over the odds of seven come eleven until two o'clock each morning, then stumbled on deck and crawled around in the darkness wailing, "George? Hey, George, didja save us a place?" I often suspected George of deliberately hiding himself; at least I never heard his friends find him, but then I always went right back to sleep after they stepped on my face. Another deterrent to risking one's life on the open deck was the ship's crew, who showed up shortly after four each morning and proceeded to wash down the deck with a fire hose. Also any stray bodies that happened to be lying around. True, their attentions got me up in time for two breakfasts.

Chiefly, during the day, we had nothing to do but amuse ourselves. Now and then there were some half-hearted attempts at calisthenics, but nobody, including the officers, took much interest. We read a good deal and talked endlessly about what combat would be like, what home had been like, what was wrong with the Army (a subject too big for adequate discussion during the Duration and six months, we decided), and what we had heard or overheard during the past twenty-four hours. Somebody had invariably gleaned that "we are now passing through the most dangerous waters of the Pacific." There was also considerable discussion as to just where we would be if and when we "arrived safely." Mostly we favored Australia but nobody with authority had ever said that definitely, so at various times we were just as sure it would be New Zealand, Hawaii, India, New Caledonia, the Fijiis, or Port Moresby.

Eventually a bulletin came down on "Australian Currency and Customs." Our destination thus decided, we learned what we could from this bulletin and a lot of other things (that might have been condensed into another bulletin titled "How Are the Women?") from the ship's stewards. Most of

this latter information, though highly entertaining, was not necessarily accurate in every detail.

If we weren't reading or talking there were a variety of games, furnished, I think, by the Red Cross. These included everything from Old Maid and Double Deck Pinochle to Puzzle Peg and Monopoly, all of which can be played for money. Six of us, during the course of the voyage, played 981 hands of Hearts for "the drinks," which, I am sorry to say, I still owe. Another group (they must have been non-coms with no details to bother about) played nearly five hundred rubbers of bridge. If two guys at any time found room for their feet and a pair of dice, they started a crap game.

There was a canteen, aft on "C" deck, at the other end of a long line of guys some of whom had been waiting since the last run to Bordeaux in the spring of 1917. It sold various things at prices nicely adjusted to more than take care of our twenty-per-cent increase in pay. Now and then a couple of us, in lieu of a cash donation, would storm this canteen and return with several bottles of warm Pepsi-Cola.

TROOPS CANTEEN

Every afternoon, promptly at three o'clock, we "abandoned ship." With all our heart and soul the first week, and a firm conviction that were this one the "real thing," *we* would get into a boat as quickly as possible and let somebody else be the heroes. Later, as we continued to plow serenely along with never a sign of a periscope, some grew bored with the whole business and would disappear into the nearest

men's room at two-fifty-five sharp, remaining there until the "all clear" sounded. But I could never quite manage that degree of fatalism, having little or no desire to die, of all places, in a bathtub. The sailors who attended these drills were bored beyond words. At first they derived a certain amount .

of pleasure out of telling some particularly pale soldier, "Don't worry, Buddy, yu c'n allas grab a pail and bail out a foxhole." (This joke, I think, was first uttered by Lief the Lucky in 090.) As we grew pretty fed up ourselves we retorted with another classic (credited to Eric the Red, 097), "Aw, take a week off an' float around." That ended our relations with the crew.

Each evening, the speaker system rasped, "All troops. Attention. All doors, ports, and windows will be closed and secured immediately. There will be no more smoking on the open deck." Three or four of us would take a smokeless turn on the open deck. Often, as a mild form of amusement, we would count the other ships in our convoy. This, at times, could be disconcerting. Here and there along the way we seemed to pick up boats, usually at night, and on counting the ships next evening we would get eight where there should have been ten, or twenty where there should have been eighteen. We could never be quite sure but what that extra ship had a Rising Sun in her flag locker or logged her books in the year 2600. It was food for lying awake.

After crossing the equator we used to while away another half hour looking for the Southern Cross, which we found four times, in four different places, and four in-no-way-similar shapes. There is still considerable disagreement among us as to just what the Southern Cross looks like and where the hell do you look if it does. And we watched the Big Dipper as it gradually slid down the northern sky, finally leaving us flat somewhere in the vicinity of latitude 65.

On Sundays we of the faith held church services on the starboard side, forward, while those who put their trust in luck and the efficiency of the Matson Line told dirty jokes on the port side. Usually, however, the services were well attended, there being an amazing number of young men who became deeply and suddenly religious on finding the nearest land two miles away, straight down.

While en route we received two letters, which wasn't at all bad considering the kind of rural route we were living on. One, from the Commanding General, was of a type, and assured us that Higher Headquarters felt no qualms concerning our fortitude, courage etc., and added that "troopships are not built for comfort." A truth that we held to be quite and sufficiently self-evident. The other, from President Roosevelt, stating that *he* felt no qualms concerning our fortitude, courage etc., either, and was "with us in spirit," excited a mild sort of interest and elicited several ribald remarks. All of us were damn well pleased really, to think that somebody somewhere had gone to the bother of preparing so many "letters from the President" for our consumption; and we felt, deep down, (and somewhat deeper among the Democrats) that what it said was probably true enough and the President *did* have a personal interest in us. But you can't let the guy on the next bunk know you feel like that.

About the time that "abandoning ship" had become just another formation, and even the hard-boiled-egg gag was wearing a little thin, and our game of Hearts was fast becoming a chore rather than amusement, we crossed the International Date Line. One day it was Wednesday, the next day it was Friday. (Or, if you like it better this way, one day it was Thursday and the same day it was Friday.) This crossing cheered us considerably. It more or less definitely spotted just where we were and meant, it seemed, that the worst was behind us.

It meant something else too. The day that was Friday (or the P.M. of the day that had been Thursday) a Sergeant Rubitkish, who slept in the bunk below mine, became so excited he nearly fell out of this bunk in his hurry to tell us what he'd just figured out.

"Look," he said, "they're payin' us fur thirty-one days this month, ain't they? But we're only puttin' in time for THIRTY!"

Somebody said yes, but so what? Coming home they would get their day back.

"Yeah," said Sergeant Rubitkish, secure in the knowledge that we couldn't lose, "but coming home there won't be so many of us."

36

(This paragraph has been added for the special benefit of other soldiers who may go overseas.) Yes, some of us were seasick. Our trip was very smooth, the ocean being referred to at all times by the crew as a "lily pond" or "a puddle," but still, some of us were seasick. I was not. I ate three meals (at least three meals) every day. There were a few days when these meals did not appeal to me a great deal, but they amounted to something more than half my pay at the time, and it was too much like losing a dollar to miss one. For a while cigarettes didn't taste very good either, and I could scarcely smoke as many as I could bum in a good day's bumming, but that was all. Other soldiers, soldiers whose stomachs weren't conditioned as mine was conditioned, thanks to three years in a fraternity house, were noticeably seasick. They were afraid they would die, afraid they wouldn't die, and recovered, in that order. Seasickness, like wavy hair, is something you either have or you haven't. Thinking about it won't help.

IT HAPPENED at four o'clock one afternoon. Somebody mooning along the rail snapped his spine like a jitterbug hearing the call of Benny's clarinet, bugged his eyes like a Ripley Odditorium character, gurgled, "LAND!" Two thousand other guys said, "WHERE?" and jammed the rail till the rivets cracked.

It was land all right. Low and brown and a good ways off, but land. Dry land! A few minutes later somebody else saw a light and said so, much as Columbus' lookout must have said the same thing. It was a very dim light and like children with a new toy, we amused ourselves pointing it out to those who couldn't find it. "See! There! Look where I'm pointing. See it? It flashes!" was heard pretty steadily until well past midnight. I slept on deck, waking at four o'clock as happy as a lark (considering the hour) to find that more land or at least another light had put in an appearance.

All morning we were well within sight of land and occasionally even a house. We watched it all intently, hanging over the rail like so many vultures. One vulture, the envied possessor of a pair of field glasses, was finally rewarded. "Cripes!" he yelled, in the manner of a man who had almost forgotten such things existed, "There's a GIRL!" He went

down fighting under the weight of a dozen other soldiers who "wanted to see them glasses next." The bolder spirits took off their life belts.

We docked shortly after two. Everybody—and I mean *everybody*—jammed the rail until the boys who got there first were three feet over the ship's side but too crowded to fall. On the dock were perhaps three dozen Australian soldiers (we knew they were Australians by their hats), assorted officers, sundry longshoremen, some girls in uniform, evidently drivers, and several other girls in tight sweaters (which isn't a bad uniform either) carrying signs: "Don't Talk! The Enemy Listens!" A sort of welcoming committee, we gathered, and very welcome they were too. We ignored the signs, upwards of three thousand soldiers immediately making all the remarks—appropriate and otherwise—that they could think of on the spur of the moment.

The first thing we heard, from one of the soldiers, was the question: "Are you Yanks?"

"You're damn right we're Yanks!" we told him.

That settled, everybody yelled in chorus, "Yu gotta smoke, Yank?" They met us at the dock and they've been with us ever since.

But that afternoon we were friends with the whole world, or anyway with Australia. Somebody threw a cigarette overboard, somebody else threw a package, practically everybody threw a package. Followed a little scene on the dock that would have done the heart of Mr. R.J. Reynolds a world of good. Privates, sergeants, officers to the rank of major, long-

shoremen, Australian womanhood, in or out of uniform, all dropped what they were doing (which was staring at us, mostly) and scattered after those cigarettes like ants on their way to a picnic. Presently they threw us some of their cigarettes, which were smaller and harder than our own and while hardly as foul a substitute for tobacco as the ship's stewards had claimed they would be, still not a smoke that I would walk a mile for. Or even two feet.

Following the smokes, we threw money. I had arrived with the rather small sum of ten cents, salvaged out of a blackjack game and earmarked for one last package of Camels. But the spirit of the afternoon got me. Recklessly I threw it overboard, receiving in return what I presumed to be a coin, about the size of a quarter, with a kangaroo on one side and His Majesty George the Fifth on the other. I suspected at the time that I was money ahead, but wasn't sure about it for a week and am still a little hazy about how much.

All this merriment ceased abruptly when the speaker system rasped that "no more cigarettes or money will be thrown overboard, nor will troops communicate further with persons on the dock." Which reminded us that essentially this was still a business trip and Uncle Sam was still paying the freight. Nevertheless, we stayed on deck, and speaker system to the contrary, communicated further with persons on the dock. Far enough, at least, to find out where we were and how big the place was; that intoxicating beverages, wine and beer in quantity and Scotch too, in lesser quantities, could be had for what, it seemed to us, was a very reasonable price; and that it was late fall instead of spring. We inquired too, about "the women"; but the Diggers, talkative enough on the subject of wine and beer, became suddenly reticent on the subject of girls—sensing, I think, that we were potentially a stiff brand of competition and deciding we could damn well find out for ourselves.

Sometime that day there must have been a supper, but I don't remember it and feel pretty sure that I didn't eat it. After dark we on board ship and various shadowy persons on the dock sang songs. We sang "Deep in the Heart of Texas," and they sang something rollicking yet sad about "They sa-ay there's a troopship that's leaving Bombay. . . . Bless 'em all, the long and the short and the tall. . . . Bless 'em all!" Then we all joined in and butchered "Roll Out the Barrel," the "Pack Up Your Troubles" of World War II.

Thus we arrived safely at destination. The place had a name, certainly, but that is probably a Military Secret, and besides, as far as we were concerned that town was and always will be simply "Destination."

DEBARKATION

THROUGHOUT THE EVENING of our arrival various people with stripes and bars dashed thither and yon rescinding each other's orders as to who was getting off and who was staying aboard and what time. Everybody else was trying to pack, a practically impossible feat when there are eight men in the same stateroom. Personal equipment had become hopelessly jumbled in our weeks together. Harold, who'd been sharing his mess kit with a guy in the next stateroom, discovered that he was on the point of going ashore—in a strange land —without any utensils. He careened through the halls for fifteen minutes screaming, "Green! Hey, Green! You got my knife an' fork! Whatcha do with my knife an' fork?" Green, it developed, had packed them up and departed an hour earlier, so Harold went ashore—in a strange land—without any utensils and badgered the rest of us for three weeks for the loan of a tool. The supply sergeant took pity eventually, and issued him a brand-new set of aluminum tableware, but in the meantime Harold had learned to get along amazingly well with nothing but a spoon and never really used his knife or fork again. (He could stir his coffee with the handle and cut meat with the edge and butter his bread with his fingers.)

Personally I got along pretty well with my packing. Having parked my barracks bag near the door the night we'd come aboard, I'd left it there for the duration of the voyage, just where every tired soldier that came into our stateroom could—and did—conveniently drop on it. On one occasion Air-do Poo-poo, a decidedly paunchy character, sat on it for nearly two hours while regaling us with chapters in his unpurged version of the Louisiana Maneuvers. It had also served as a seat during 981 hands of Hearts. Thus, on arrival, my barracks bag had all the verve and general appearance of an old and battered sparring partner, but it was certainly "packed," with plenty of room on top for such odds and ends as I had to add.

After packing everything we could find room for, including several towels which were *not* turned in to the steward but kept in fond remembrance of our pleasant journey via the Matson Line (and because they were damn good towels, something soldiers never have enough of) we kicked everything else under the bunks and lugged ourselves and our baggage out into the hall. Where a lieutenant met us and told us we weren't going to debark that night after all. It was then eleven-thirty. We went to bed in disgust and our clothes and tried to sleep while the winchmen already unloading the forward hold swore at each other and dropped things, including medium tanks, on the dock from a height of forty feet. Shortly after twelve a sergeant woke us up and told us, "C'mon, we gotta get off this goddamn boat before somebody changes their mind again."

So-o, we moved out into the hall again and sat there for a time, then shuffled upstairs and sat on the deck for a considerably longer time, then lurched downstairs and waited while another company filed past, and finally, at long last,

shortly after two-thirty, we staggered down the gangplank. The thrill of arriving safely at destination was lost on me. I tripped coming down the gangplank, arriving safely on my face, a fraction of a second ahead of and directly beneath my barracks bag, which had apparently decided in advance to land on the same bit of foreign soil that I did.

Arrived, somewhat dazed but otherwise safely enough, I got to my feet and stumbled along with the rest. Presently we entered a large bare warehouse and sat down to another session of what somebody had once told me was the worst part of a war: "Not the fighting, but the sitting and waiting." While we sat a lieutenant hacked his way through the Company Roster, calling roll, the "new men" answering "Here, Sir," and the "old men" answering with something that sounded like "Yowp!" Nobody, it developed (to the intense gratification of our lieutenant, I sincerely hope) had stayed on the boat or tried to desert while crossing the dock.

The train we were waiting for showed up around a quarter to four with an advanced case of asthma and eight cars, straight out of "Union Pacific." We loaded, some wit saying, "This elevator is authorized to carry fourteen persons," and after a certain amount of trouble succeeded in lighting one of the weird little gas lamps that shone somewhat dimmer than a good deed in this naughty world. Its feeble illumination helped some in distinguishing the seats from the seatees until word came down that we would travel black-out.

That was easier ordered than accomplished. Too long had we lived with the softening influences of civilization, among them the electric light, which is extinguished by a simple flick of the wrist or by jamming a penny in the fuse box. Weird little gas lamps are something else again. We blew at it, to no effect, and turned various knobs and valves both ways, also to no effect. Gradually, as the other cars somehow put their lights out of commission, ours began to shine—or at

least show up—like a lighthouse. Outside somebody was yelling, "Turn that goddamn light off!" We discussed the possibilities of a violent explosion if we tore the whole thing bodily out of the ceiling. Finally Big Swede, whose face could best afford mangling by such an explosion, stood on a seat,

took a deep breath, and neatly blew the mantle to smithereens. We closed the globe with the aid of a flashlight and settled down to wait for the violent explosion. It never came, probably because there wasn't that much pressure in the whole system.

Eventually, after wheezing and gasping to an extent that must have necessitated artificial respiration on the part of the engineer, our train got under way and slid swiftly through the darkness at something well under fifteen miles an hour. It was too dark to see anything through the windows. Probably there wasn't anything to see anyway. And just once more I would have liked to ride on something that didn't rock or rattle or bump or sway. Still, I slept as best I could. I woke up twice, once when Harold kicked me in the stomach and once when somebody's rifle fell on my neck. At neither time did I feel anything at all like the soldier you see on the enlistment posters. I was tired and sleepy. My knees were stiff and my neck hurt. There was a draft. I don't like drafts. In fact, I suffer from an almost psychopathic fear of drafts, having had a peculiarly lasting experience with one not so long ago. What I'm trying to say is: I WANTED TO GO HOME!

That's the way I felt. But I knew too, that had some little green jinni popped up at the moment, rubbed our defunct gaslight, and said, "You can go home now," I would *not* have accepted his offer. In the Army, whether you like 'em or not, the guys that you're with, you don't let 'em down. Not when the blue chips are in.

Now AND THEN some motherly old soul has asked me, "And what did you first think of Australia?"

Usually I've given her a flimsy little story about, "Oh, it isn't much different from home, nice enough, though somewhat damper then I expected." Actually I should resort to blasphemy.

I came something less then halfway out of a sound sleep when our train stopped with a smash and a crash that suggested we had fallen through a trestle; sat up in time to get hit on the head with somebody's helmet as it fell off the baggage rack; gathered my belongings together and stumbled off the train. The sun either hadn't come up yet or wasn't going to come up. Everything looked gray. In front of us was a concrete loading ramp and a yellowish picket fence that screamed "RAILROAD PROPERTY." Somebody prodded us down the ramp and through the fence to where a row of

.. Reprinted from the September Book-of-the-Month Club News ...

c/o POSTMASTER

By CORPORAL THOMAS ST. GEORGE

WHEN a number of young men were routed out of a California barracks at five a. m. one spring day in 1942 they were pretty sure they were going back to Iowa. But unexpected things happened. First there wasn't time to sort out several truck loads of equipment and damp laundry: each man had to grab an approximate fit (one soldier never did find any shoes to fit, and was still doing K.P. in bedroom slippers months later because he couldn't hike). Then those ominous postal cards adressed to "Next of Kin" had to be signed, bearing the laconic message, "Arrived Safely at Destination." When they were told their mail address would be c/o Postmaster, San Francisco, they knew they were bound overseas.

Their destination was "Australia" and, perhaps, the unconscious hero of this modest and humorous chronicle is Australia itself. This is one of the first testimonies of what has happened to the average American boys who went "Down Under." In the Digger's own phrase, most of the Yanks took a fairly dim view, at first, of Australian comforts and resources. It was something of a revelation to them that there are parts of the world where plumbing and ice cream and 100 per cent hamburgers are not universally available. But little by little, through Corporal St. George's informal narrative, as frank as a letter home, we see the Yanks realizing the hospitality and enduring temper of their accidental hosts.

There must have been plenty of opportunity, if our Australian friends were sensitive, to be scandalized by the high spirits (and high pay) of these visitors. Hanging out of the carriage windows of the suburban train we hear them roaring in unison their echo of the sturdy and elderly station mistress: "Tike 'er into Central Stition!" The good woman is still wondering what amused them. Or the whistles and halloos of homage directed toward every younger Australian female may well have been irksome to A. I. F. veterans who were back from two years hard slogging in Africa. They had no spare uniforms to show and little money for buying. But both the kindly temper of the Australians and the quick adaptability of the Yanks shine through this report.

Corporal St. George gives a good picture of a voyage in convoy, in one of the former Matson Liners which many of us remember. But what is more novel, and first in its field, is the detailed and jovial account of American troops in Australian camps. They had supposed because they were so far south the weather would be warm. To their dismay they found it was winter "Down Under," and a wet one. They lived in tin "'uts" and were appalled at the lack of drinking fountains, hot showers, screened windows, and cots for sleeping. For bedding they filled burlap bags with lumps of straw, and at mess they encountered the immortal Australian mutton. More frightful still, it was some time before their supply of cokes caught up with them: they had to drink "koala beer." When they looked for a latrine, their hosts said, "Oh, you mean the bloody lavat'ry— it's that little tin 'ut with pipes on it." The movies they saw were very ancient indeed, but they whistled and stamped at the briefest glimpse of any silk-clad female leg crossing the screen. The worthy Diggers thought the Yank's training camp was pretty luxurious—"a bloody resort plice," they called it—but that may have been a touch of their grim humor.

This is an extraordinarily attractive book. It gives an account both comic and humane of two quite different democracies, shaken together and learning to pull in harness. There isn't an atom of lip service or hypocrisy of any kind, either in the author's unvarnished narrative or in the behavior of the Australians he describes. There is in full bubble the peculiarly buoyant humor that we like to think of as American.

Australian Army trucks stood waiting. A brawny Digger grabbed my barracks bag, heaved it into a truck, said something that sounded like, " 'Ere Oi Aye Mite, givee a 'and," and before I could say anything, lifted me more or less by one foot and heaved me in after my barracks bag, slammed the endgate, shouted something else that sounded like, "Hoi! She's roight, Mite!" in the general direction of the cab, and leaped clear as our driver hurled us forward in a manner that suggested he wanted to take off.

For perhaps forty-five minutes we were hurled along a narrow black-top road in a way that made our own drivers, by comparison, look like so many spinsters out with the new electric auto. We passed one rather oldish customer pedaling a bicycle and yelled at him, "How far t' town?" He answered nothing, only dropped his jaw and stared at us and all but fell off his bicycle. We decided he probably thought we were Japanese invasion troops up to our old trick of using English phrases. Somebody dropped a cigarette among the barracks bags at this stage of the game, and we ignored the remainder of the countryside while dealing with the efforts of this would-be arsonist. And *that* was my first impression of Australia. Now that I think of it, I should better, when asked, go right ahead and blaspheme.

Fate being with us, we lived to detruck in the middle of what was to be, for a time at least, "home." Our particular home being one of a number of tin buildings, each some eighty feet long, that the rural members of the organization immediately decided to call "pig sheds." Us city fellers, unable to make such comparisons, figured they were barracks, but learned instead that they were "huts." A hut, we gathered, being any building other than a home or a place of business, the word not necessarily referring to either the size or the method of construction. All right, so we lived in huts.

But we were accustomed to living in barracks with insulation over our heads, thermostats at our beck and call, hot showers under the same roof, screened windows, and fancy iron cots. And we were mildly stunned at the appearance of our huts, which had not one of these necessities of life. If the windows were open, anything up to the size of a large duck could—and sometimes did—fly in and out. The windows shut, we were bothered by nothing larger than the sparrows that came through the gaps under the eaves. We inquired

about insulation, but the Diggers who composed the camp complement confused our pronunciation with "installation" and described at length the wonders of their brand-new sewage disposal plant. Which may have been a very nice installation indeed but added practically nothing to the warmth or comfort of our huts.

And instead of fancy iron cots our huts provided plenty of reasonably soft flooring. We stood around wondering as to just how much good three blankets would do under the circumstances, but it turned out things weren't to be quite as rugged as all that. Somebody stuck his head in the door and yelled we should all go down to the QM hut and draw beds. Considerably cheered, we all took off for the QM hut. There we learned that what we were getting were not exactly beds but large burlap bags which we might fill with baled straw to our hearts' content. Various soldiers who fancied they were quite witty made the usual remarks regarding hay rides and admitted (over and over) that *they* had always favored a quick "roll in the hay." Others, who were susceptible to hay fever, failed to see the humor of the situation. Though I took only the softest straw I could find, I continued to wake up every morning for a week firmly convinced and ready to accuse the man next to me of baling it again while I slept.

Immediately following our authorized possession of the Australian version of a Beauty-Rest mattress and two thick woolen blankets, we went to breakfast. Most of us, I'm afraid, were looking forward to large helpings of ham and eggs, our

usual reward for a night's activity. Instead we had coffee made with chicory (a coarse kind of gravel) and our first lesson in the anatomy of the sheep, as found in mutton stew. Thick was this stew, like cold glue, full of unidentifiable vegetables, and with all the delicious appeal of a soggy snowbank.

After breakfast we gathered in our hut. Spotlight (Spotlight was a sergeant who had once, in his youth, played part of a season of pro football and was wont to recount, with the slow-motion camera of his mind, a play-by-play account of that season during which he met and dropped most of the stars of the past ten years—hence his nickname)—well, Spotlight sought some rather vital information, "Say," he asked one of the Diggers who was with us, "Where's the latrine?"

"Aye?" said the Digger, looking even blanker than Spotlight.

"The latrine," Spotlight repeated, "you know. . . . Where—"

"Oi!" said the Digger, a great light breaking over his face "You means the bloody lavatory! Down the street, Mite, roight to the end, an' acrosst the paddock. You'll see 'er. She's a little 'ut, wit pipes on. An' 'ere, Mite (Spotlight was leaving), you better tike me newspiper. . . ."

Indeed, we were in a strange land.

IT LOOKED SOMEWHAT less strange and considerably brighter after the sun came out along about ten o'clock. By that time a good fifty per cent of the outfit had "snided-off," that is, left in the general direction of a town without informing the first sergeant or anybody else as to either their plans or where-abouts. We new men, being unaccustomed to such goings on, went in search of the Top-Kick to see would it be all right if we left, and were pleasantly surprised to find that that gentle-man had snided-off himself shortly after nine o'clock.

Thus assured that nobody was checking, we took off our-selves, inquired directions of a friendly Digger (rewarding him, on request, with a Yankee cigarette) and tramped two miles over a series of tiny fields to the nearest town. Where we saw, among others, the regimental commander. Possibly he had only come to be with his troops, who were certainly there in strength.

Town was a little place, about the size to support six gas stations back home. Itself it had but one, obviously long out of business, that advertised "petrol" and "motor spirit" in-

stead of gasoline, though claiming for this petrol and motor spirit the same colossal feats that gasoline can admittedly perform regardless of the temperature. We learned, presently, that it wasn't a gas station at all, for that matter, but a 'petrol bowser." We learned too, and quite rapidly, that rather than ask for a bar we should inquire the whereabouts of a "pub" or hotel; unless the people we were asking appeared sufficiently worldly, then we might safely inquire was there a "sly grog shop" in the vicinity. That first afternoon, however, it was scarcely necessary to inquire anything. The town boasted but one hotel, and it had been found—with or without inquiry—by upwards of eight hundred Yanks, of which some two hundred had succeeded in penetrating to the Public Room.

This was a small room, flanked by a bar that had no stools, with a fireplace instead of a juke box, and posters on the walls that advertised the next running of the Grand National Surrey Race or something instead of Henry Bussey's Saturday appearance at the Marigold Ballroom. On shelves behind the bar were perhaps a bare dozen bottles of various shapes and sizes. One of us (a Harvard man) pointed out that such an array was "English" and not to be confused with the vulgar displays of quantities of bottles usually found in American bars. Another soldier (no Harvard man, he) asked scornfully of the bar tender, "Is that all yu' *got?*"

The bar tender, poor man, didn't attempt an answer. He didn't have time. More or less feebly assisted by three nondescript females he scattered up and down the bar in a vain but valiant effort to cope with such unprecedented rush of business. Undoubtedly he had never seen anything like it before in all his life. To make matters worse, he must needs change dollars and cents to pounds and shillings with every transaction, a task with which he was mentally unfitted to cope himself so continually referred to one of the females. The one who was bright enough to tell innumerable soldiers—whether truthfully or not, I couldn't say—that she was a married woman, the wife of a large man with a violent temper who might wander into the bar at any moment.

We succeeded, finally, in obtaining a glass of something which the Harvard man claimed was "old ale" and the label insisted was "XXXX Bitter Beer." I decided it was certainly bitter if nothing else, and went off in search of some ice cream with a soldier who had last thought of the English in connection with the Boston Tea Party. Our connoisseur of "old ale" stayed in the pub and eventually became quite drunk in a manner that left some doubt as to the exact advantages of a Harvard education after all.

We illiterates soon found a store, or rather a shop, and asked for some ice cream. A small boy, already the proud and envied owner of a U.S. fatigue hat that covered him down to his shoulders, volunteered the information that what we wanted was "an ice." Whatever it was, ice or ice cream, we took some and paid for it (how much we paid we didn't have the slightest idea). The taste didn't quite measure up to American standards, being more like sherbet than genuine ice cream, but still we managed three large bowls apiece, to the undisguised admiration of our small friend under the hat. In fact, he watched us closely with glazed eyes, and hung out his tongue until we bought him a dish.

Like the hotel, the shop was jammed solid with assorted Yanks, all buying feverishly of the limited stock of goodies. We quickly learned that candy (of a hard variety, but the only variety available) wasn't candy at all, but "lollies"; that cookies were a type of young lady (not the best type, we gathered), small round edible dainties being strictly "biscuits"; that "Aw, break it down" meant "Who do you think you're kidding?"; and that a shilling was a "bob" and wouldn't go as far as two bits. Like the owner of the pub, the young ladies who ran the establishment were completely overwhelmed at the rush of business and hopelessly uninformed as to the present rate of exchange. Simple country lasses, they were probably more confused and inefficient than usual when confronted with so many strange young men speaking what must have sounded to them a very strange language, and all obviously intent on leaping the counter to lay violent hands on their persons. They blushed furiously, admitted they were seventeen and nineteen respectively, but declined (at least while we were present) to divulge their names. (Three weeks later these same country lasses, simple no longer, could take a Yank or leave him alone.)

On leaving the shop we wandered further through the town. The natives seemed friendly enough but somewhat reserved and kept pretty much to themselves, content to smile and wave at us from doorways and behind hedges. Nowhere did we see any men except a few very old codgers and one Minister of the Gospel. Immediately after sundown the town closed up, blacked-out, and as far as we could tell, everybody went to bed. There being nothing much else to do we started back to camp.

As we were leaving the main street half a dozen little boys cornered us. "Souvenir?" they screamed. "Souvenir, Yank? Yu' got any 'Merican money? Give us a cigarette, willya, Yank?" We gave them the last of our American

pennies and part of a package of Old Golds. Well, we thought, maybe the populace didn't meet us with open arms exactly, like the French met our old men when they hit Le Havre with the first A.E.F., but we were giving away pennies, weren't we? Besides, us Anglo-Saxons are naturally more reserved.

Swinging along through the twilight we might have sung "The Yanks Are Coming" except that the Army, when it sings these days, favors ballads or something loud and lewd. We worked on "I Don't Wanna Set the Wor-r-r-rld on Fire."

SOMEWHERE IN AUSTRALIA

THE SNIDE-OFFS began to trickle home late Sunday afternoon, full of lurid tales concerning their week-end adventures in a strange land. It was generally agreed that the girls were plentiful enough and friendly, that of most of the other necessities of life there was a definite shortage; and that being a Yank was a strong point in a guy's favor.

At Reveille Monday we took up the slack and went back to routine, the supposedly deadly routine of the army. We didn't find it particularly deadly. During our rather extended troop movement we had lived more or less from hour to hour, never quite knowing what the next hour might bring. It was a relief really to know that we would spend Monday forenoon listening to a subnormal corporal's confusing lecture on the intricacies of the EE8A field telephone; that Tuesday afternoon we would hike; that Thursday morning would be devoted to the "Identification of Japanese

Aircraft"; that Saturday afternoon we might wander through the countryside on our own. We discovered, Tuesday afternoon, that weeks of soft living had done nothing for our physical condition. We discovered too, that though we might be overseas and far from the watchful eyes of the War Department, we were still soldiers and must dress accordingly. We dug air-raid shelters and occasionally suffered a practice but total black-out (both of which, it seemed, meant that we were at least reasonably close to the Theater of Operations), but we still laced the shoes we weren't wearing and hung our clothes as prescribed by little charts that appeared twice weekly, never in the same form.

Nor did Spotlight, when he woke us up each morning for Reveille, seem to realize that we were on the verge of giving our lives that democracy might survive. His was still the manner of a man firmly convinced that we were the kind of guys who would cheerfully stay in bed till we rotted and democracy crashed about our heads unless he, Spotlight, got us up. He spoke to us accordingly, in a loud roar. The natives may have recognized us, for a time, as the Saviors of Australia, but not Spotlight. Now and then, thanks to Spotlight and others like him, we could almost forget that we were ten thousand miles from home and imagine we were "somewhere in Kansas" instead of Australia. But never for very long. Things were continually cropping up that, while they may not have shown us just how *far* from home we were, made it quite plain that we weren't in the good old U.S.A.

For instance, a short distance from camp was a farm that owned and operated two kangaroos. We passed their paddock regularly on our hikes and at first seldom failed to compare them with the various odd beasts that are supposed to torment soldiers afflicted with acute alcoholism. Later, in spite of the evidence, we would all insist "they ain't no such animal"; and accusing Finney (a notorious sot) of being the only one who could see them, tell him he should explain away their presence as best he could. But all in all they seemed to prove, definitely, that we were *not* in Fort Leonard Wood, Mo.

Besides the 'roos (as we presently learned to call them) there were a lot of other things that served to remind us we were something more than forty miles out of St. Louis, few of which were in any way as amusing as our spring-powered friends. Briefly, most of the items we had always thought of in the States as being "necessities," became, suddenly, "luxuries." Coca-Cola was little more than a memory. Instead, did we become desperate enough, we went to the Australian canteen and drank Koala Beer, an alleged soft drink that tasted like warm strawberry pop less the fizz, was bottled by the quart, and sealed with a rubber stopper that defied the efforts of three strong men to open it. There were other drinks (soft), sarsaparilla and ginger beer, that tasted like

nothing in particular, and something the natives called "lemonide" that resembled mineral water.

But drinking anything at the Australian canteen involved a certain amount of trouble. It opened only at irregular intervals between inventories, being even worse than our own canteens in this respect; it was stocked to meet the Australian purse ("Bloody five bob a die, I gets, less the bloody dependency for my old woman!") and appetite ("Gimme a bloody riser blide, Mite, the Yank 'ere'll pie for me pot."); and it was run by veterans of the A.I.F. Returned, men who refused to recognize that we were a mechanized army and continued to move around at a top speed of about four miles an hour. Eventually some of our own misfits were detailed to work in the canteen. Whether or not their addition improved the service any was open to question. They were inclined to sell what could be sold considerably faster, but lost all the time they gained while trying to figure the change (in shillings and pence) on a five-pound note; this being practically impossible when neither customer nor clerk knew what it was all about.

Between seven and eight-thirty each evening, Monday through Friday, the canteen did break down and grudgingly dispense with a small quantity of beer. Actually laying hands

on a beer, however, was something else. First a man stood in line up to forty-five minutes that he might purchase "beer tickets" (two per man per trip). Then he went inside and stood in line for a glass. Finally, if there was time, he stood

in line for a beer (one per man per trip) and if he pushed hard enough and hollered loud enough and had a close friend behind the bar, he got his beer and crawled back to a

table and drank it. At first, thanks to this system and the acute shortage of glasses, it was a little difficult to become really drunk.

Yankee ingenuity soon fixed that. Somebody found that non-drinkers could be seduced with ice-cream bars and sent off to buy beer tickets for their friends; another genius discovered we could obtain half-pint bottles of milk, drink the milk, then use the bottles for beer, and the problem was solved. The hardier spirits made quite a point of this milk angle, either begging someone else to drink the stuff for them or, in extreme cases, going so far as to pour it out the window that they might sooner have beer. As for me, beer in a half-pint bottle looked too much like a urinalysis for my taste. I went into business strictly as a milk-bottle-emptier and put on fifteen pounds.

Cigarettes were never a problem. A benevolent Uncle Sam (and the United States Army Service Forces) saw to it that we received one package a day (issue) until our own canteen opened. Bumming, in the meantime, was *severely* frowned on. Once or twice I was reduced to buying a pack of Australian cigarettes, which, among other things, were decidedly more expensive than our own. Why, I certainly don't know.

By way of amusement there were a few battered Western magazines that had survived the trip and a daily newspaper. This newspaper was considerably more interested in (and so devoted considerably more space to) the possibilities of various horses winning various races and the wonderful spirit of sacrifice that enabled a country to struggle along on three Race Days a month, than in how the war was coming along. Especially for our benefit the newspaper presently instituted a "Home News for U.S. Forces" column, which consisted of possibly two dozen lines of type and brought us, hot off the press, so to speak, such items as: "200 Strike in War Plant," "Bandits Kill 3 in Chicago," "Lana Turner Seeks Divorce," "Gas Rationing Hinted," "New York Murder Baffles Police," "Errol Flynn Faces Charges," "Georgia Adopts Electric Chair," "Actor Pleads Dependency," "Saboteurs To Die," "Rooney Marriage Null," and last week's baseball scores. We knew what was going on.

Our camp boasted one theater, a tin building seating about five hundred or something less than ten per cent of the available personnel, that insisted on showing double features, this being the Australian idea of a big night. Some of the movies, or rather, "pictures," we had seen; others were vaguely remembered by nobody except a couple of World War I veterans who were likewise playing a return engagement. We

were considerably surprised and somewhat impressed the first few times we attended the pictures to find that it was a breach of etiquette to rush the exits immediately the fadeout appeared on the screen. Instead, it seemed, we must wait and stand at a kind of attention (only easing towards the exits) while "God Save the King" blurred through the public-address system and colored slides of President Roosevelt, General Douglas MacArthur, a third character with a prominent jaw that we variously decided was John Curtin, General Sir Thomas Blamey, the Viceroy (if there was a Viceroy), or the winner of the Grand National Lottery, and finally George the VI (who, in that company, appeared as the chinless wonder) flashed on the screen. It wasn't too hard to remember that we were ten thousand miles from home when we saw our leaders (in technicolor) instead of "Next Week's Jackpot —$200."

Our truck drivers in particular could scarcely forget it. Within Camp Limits they still drove pretty much as they were accustomed to (down the middle, hell for leather, veering to the right when avoiding accidents) but on leaving the Main Gate they were immediately subject—in addition to the military ruling that prohibited excessive speeds, which they ignored—to the customs of the native drivers, which they could *not* ignore. (That is, our drivers could not ignore them. The native population could and did ignore everything but the law of gravity when out tooling their autos along the highway.) So our transportation platoon learned to drive "by the left"; fought an impulse to scream, "Get yu own sidda the road!" at every car they met; and continued to go to pieces when confronted with an automobile in which it appeared that somebody was riding but nobody was driving. Many a driver, both Aussie and Yank, took to a shoulder, sometimes the same shoulder, those first few weeks in an effort to show in advance which side they preferred while negotiating the ticklish business of meeting.

Luckily civilian traffic was light, due to the petrol rationing. There were no serious accidents. Probably there was some considerable debate among the members of the Australian AA concerning just where the hell them bloody Yanks

learned to drive, but we didn't hear that side of the story. According to our truck drivers—and we believed them—we were in a damn strange land.

If any of us tried to forget it, our C.O. reminded us that being overseas as we were, we had a "supply problem." He suggested it would be better if we changed our socks and mended them instead of wearing them out and carrying a tale of woe to the supply sergeant in hopes of getting a new pair.

Did we still forget it, we had only to look at Reem, Robert. Reem, Robert had neglected to acquire any shoes before we left the States, had worn out his civilian shoes while we were on the boat, and had been reduced to a pair of bedroom slippers and a steady diet of K.P. and latrine orderly (because he couldn't hike) since we'd arrived in camp. At first, frankly, some of us rather envied Reem, Robert, who, through long association, became quite friendly with all the cooks and did little or nothing except eat while he was on K.P. Later, when Reem, Robert *wanted* to hike (to the nearest town) but couldn't leave camp because his bedroom slippers were not recognized as a part of the "proper uniform," we realized the true significance of our supply problem. I was glad that I had shoes—even 10-EE's.

PROBABLY THE ONLY THING that we really disliked about
our first few weeks in Australia was the weather. That we
didn't like the weather, that we thought the weather was
miserable, that the weather was interfering with our plans
and training, that the weather spoiled many a precious pass
were all bad enough; but what was worse, we couldn't write
home and complain about the weather. You see, they told us,
there are only about three places in Australia where it ever
r---s, and if you write home that it is r-----g the Japs will
know where we are. That, of course, was taboo. But, we won-
dered, if there are so goddamn many places in Australia
where it doesn't r--n, why don't we move? They told us we
mustn't worry about that. Where we moved, or didn't move,
was something G.H.Q. would decide. We had visions of
G.H.Q., diabolical monsters, all colonels no doubt, hunched

CAUTION
MILITARY SECRETS

over a report of the mean annual rainfall of Australia, gloating at the spot they'd found for us.

To add to our disgust, what mail we received, though welcome of course, added little to our appreciation of the climate. Most of our letters had been written while we were still playing Hearts on the broad expanse of the Pacific, at which time our friends knew nothing except that we had left Frisco. But did any of them imagine that we might possibly have "arrived safely" in Alaska and console us accordingly with promises of hand-knitted sweaters or useful brown mufflers? No! To a man, and to a woman, they were convinced that we had or would shortly arrive, not where it was cold and damp, but where soft tropic breezes would play softly through our hair. Some of them became positively lewd concerning our supposed existence on a secret base in the South Seas. Where clothes were sheer absurdity, dusky native lasses a necessity or a luxury depending on the point of view, and gracefully waving palm trees laced a tapestry across the sky and protected us from the glare of the tropic sun. (The above was lifted, practically intact, from *The National Geographic* and forwarded to me by a young lady with whom I immediately severed all diplomatic relations.)

The gracefully-waving-palm-tree myth had already exploded right in our faces. There were some palm trees near camp, but they didn't lace any tapestries to speak of. They stood around in the rain with the rest of us and looked cold and miserable and out of place, like nudists in a gooseberry patch. Obviously, we decided, the mere presence of palm trees does not necessarily insure a sub-tropical climate. And how I wished, those first few weeks, that Josie knew as much. Nor did these palm trees at any time protect us from the glare of a tropic sun. If one of us so much as saw a small patch of pale wintry sun, he staked a claim on it.

The natives insisted that this weather was all "very unusual," but we'd heard that before (in California, for one

place) and expected to hear it again, wherever we might go. We ignored them unless they became too insistent or too loud or harked back too far ("the winter of 1810," for instance) in their efforts to remember a similar season and convince us that the weather we were experiencing was truly an experience for all but the very oldest settlers. In fact, a phenomenon. Then we asked them, "If this is so goddamn phenomenal, why do you build your houses eight feet off the ground?"

We suffered and cursed the exigencies of the service that demanded we live through "Two winters in a row!" Our camp being more or less paved, we had no mud to contend with, only the r--n and the everlasting chill. The former (the r--n) had an ugly habit of coming at night when we were inside anyway and therefore had nothing to gain. During the day it usually held off until some optimistic lieutenant got a hike well under way, caught us with our pants down two miles from camp and drenched us till we treaded water. The everlasting chill worked a twenty-four hour shift, seven days a week, being heart and soul in somebody's War Effort, just whose we could only suspect. Particularly this chill cut us down at Reveille, and on one occasion provided the background for as macabre a bit of humor as ever appealed to Nero.

Louis, a thin shanky sort of youth, one of Spotlight's luckless platoon and the unwilling recipient of a good share of Spotlight's decidedly heavy-handed wit, was standing more or less at ease preparatory to "falling in." I say more or less. His bony shoulders were hooped against the wind, his whole attitude indicating that here was a man on the verge of collapse. Worse than that, he had his hands in his pockets, a place where "good soldiers" wouldn't be caught dead with their hands.

Spotlight, always disgustingly full of vim, verve, animal spirits, and according to most, bologna, even at 6 A.M., saw Louis, surged up to within four inches of that hapless young man's pinched face, roared, "Are you cold?"

Louis stammered y-y-yess, he was cold.

"Well," roared Louis' leader, "GET WARM!"

OUTSIDE OF THE NEW SEWAGE disposal plant (which loomed up like a squat while utilitarian mosque on the other side of the parade ground, and being less than five years old was worshiped by the natives as a living symbol of the truly great strides Australia was making in the general direction of civilization) the facilities in our camp were, to our way of thinking, all just shortly on this side of the Pleistocene Period. The camp complement (loyal Diggers all) insisted otherwise. Ours, they said, was "the best bloomin' cimpe in Australia; a bloody resort plice, that's wot she is!" By their standards maybe, she was a "bloody resort plice," but our standards were higher.

We were accustomed to individual wash bowls with gleaming chromium fixtures, glistening white enamel, and sixteen-inch mirrors, one about as good as another for seeing a face in, thanks to the daily efforts of a hard-working latrine squad. Back in the States we had shared a relatively private bath with nothing larger than a 'platoon. We'd had hot and cold running water. We'd taken for granted the presence of drinking fountains in our barracks, complained because there were only two, and agreed that shaving every day was one of the Horrors of War. Gentlemen, we didn't know what war was.

Our "bloody resort plice" didn't know what plumbing was. The drinking fountain, we soon learned, is native only to the United States and will not or does not or at least is nonexistent in Australia.

Nor did our "resort plice," tucked away in the dripping hills, have much to offer in the way of glistening white enamel or private baths. We shared our washroom, the larger of the "little tin 'uts with pipes on," with the rest of the battalion. Compared with a platoon, a battalion is a large group. We washed, after a fashion, in long tin troughs (not unlike hog troughs, the country boys said). We shaved by the light of three feeble bulbs doing their best to conserve electricity (our "little tin 'ut" had dispensed with windows, in the interests of God knows what) and without benefit of any sixteen-inch mirrors or hot water. I wrote home (naturally) describing the Horrors of War I was suffering in the interests of democracy, with hope of a little sympathy. I think it went over my family's head. Mother wrote back in an airy oh-but-think-how-things-could-be-much-worse sort of tone, and remarked that Grandfather had *always* shaved in cold water and look what a man *he* was. Which encouraged me not at all, particularly when I remembered that Grandfather had fought in another war, the Civil War, where beards were S.O.P., and had died with a flowing set of whiskers that had to be curled to fit in his coffin.

Actually we only shaved in cold water for about a week (three shaves) or until somebody discovered that there was almost always a certain amount of relatively hot water in the little stoves where we washed our mess kits. From that time on we stole this water regularly, by the helmetful, whenever we observed a disgustingly clean-shaven colonel suspiciously eyeing our own sometimes advanced cases of "five o'clock shadow." Much to the disgust of the K.P.'s, who had to haul the water some distance and were highly incensed to think they were doing such back-breaking labor mostly for the benefit of soldiers too dainty to shave in cold water. Often, of course, this mess-kit water was inclined to be somewhat greasy and something less than sparkling clear, but I didn't write home about that. I didn't want to hear how Grandfather had considered himself *lucky* could he lay hands on a little grease for an after-shave lotion. I suffered in silence, except for a certain amount of blasphemy from the K.P.'s, and learned to shave passably well without a mirror.

I learned too what fools these youngsters be who abhor a Saturday-night bath. Officially, due to a lack of bathing facilities, we were limited to one shower a week. This activity appeared on the Training Schedule as "personal hygiene"; we referred to it as, "Jeez! Hot showers!" Which was true enough, to a certain extent. The water was hot (while it lasted), but it trickled rather than showered. The bathhouse

itself was the usual little tin 'ut with pipes on and large gaps under the eaves that suggested the whole building had originally been designed as a wind tunnel. Nobody dallied while dressing and very few undressed until they had made arrangements with a friend for the immediate use of his particular shower, under which it would not be unbearably cold. Some who insisted on wandering around in the classic locker-room costume, a pair of sandals, turned quite blue. But we still snided-off for an extra shower every chance we got. (When I mentioned this fact in a letter, my family cabled for verification.) And did any of us ever think our crude bathing facilities were just too much, we could go outside where two Diggers, who stoked the boiler that warmed the water that cooled off coming through the pipes, wandered around in the shortest of shorts with never a sign of a goose pimple. They made us who were bundled to the ears feel like sissies.

Our cooks, too, went well back on their heels when first confronted with the Australian version of "cooking facilities." Most of them (the cooks, not the facilities) had served their apprenticeship in various one-arm joints where they could stand in the middle of the counter and reach everything including the drunk asleep on the pinball machine. Now, in a foreign land, they found to their dismay that what facilities there were were scattered the length and breadth of a large hut with a minimum of pipes on it. This meant that a considerable amount of water had to be carried each day, and while that didn't particularly bother the cooks, it worried hell out of the K.P.'s. Believe me.

Nor was the actual cooking done in approved White Castle style. Instead of a stove there was a large complicated boiler with a variety of attachments that had only one thing in common—what they cooked was steamed, well steamed. Our cooks, guys who had never quite mastered the intricacies of the "How To Cut Beef" manual, weren't mentally equipped to ever gather more than a faint inkling of the intricacies of "power through steam." For a time they built a fire and hoped for the best. Later somebody dug up a guy who had once been a steamfitter's assistant and put him on permanent K.P. Naturally, human nature being what it is, this young man was very backward about actually doing any

K.P., and soon acquired, for all practical purposes, the exalted standing of a "second cook," refusing to do anything except stare at the water glass now and then, with an absorbed if somewhat vacant stare. Following which, he would order one of the common K.P.'s, one who knew nothing of the wonders of steam, "Pump 'er full, Jack. I'll tell yu' when to stop." During our stay he gained twenty-two pounds, which may or may not have been an indication of anything, but served to arouse considerable suspicion.

For a few days following our arrival we lived, or rather existed, on food prepared (if you could call it that) for us by several sheep herders in uniform, disguised as cooks. The Australian Army, we decided, has no classification system comparable with our own. If a man can kill sheep and dig rutabagas and consistently look as if he just crawled off a freight train, they make him a cook. Thereafter, day in and day out, he mangles sheep and digs rutabagas and serves the Australian idea of a good hot meal—mutton stew. Which, we found, was *not* good, seldom hot, and scarcely a meal.

We did the best we could on bread and a miserable kind of bitter grapefruit marmalade, what little foodstuff the canteen had to offer, and lived for the day when Big Swede and Squawky and Stew Allen (our own cooks) went back on duty, adding corn flakes and pancakes to the menu. For several days immediately following their return to the kitchen we ate heartily and gloried in the superior performance of men trained at an American "Cooks and Bakers School." We never admitted as much to Big Swede or Squawky or Stew Allen (that being unheard of) but privately we agreed that while they were perhaps far short of Waldorf standards, it was certainly wonderful the way they could open a box of cornflakes.

Later, as usual, we complained bitterly about the food we were being served, whether or not with more grounds than usual I'm not quite sure. The coffee contained a certain percentage of chicory (about 98 per cent, we decided) and at first it tasted very foul indeed. After we'd been drinking it for a couple of weeks we thought no more about it, merely remarking now and then that such a drink would indeed dissolve the handle on a mess cup. Gradually too, we became used—or at least resigned—to the bread, which was heavier and soggier than American bread; and the powdered milk, which may be nourishing and all that as Mr. Wickard claims it to be, but is *not* the pure, sweet, Grade A milk that comes out of a cream-top bottle.

And almost to a man we gained weight. One of us, however, a guy called Big Shark, thought it was the lack of worry rather than the food that added to his waistline. Big Shark, a regrettably weak character it would seem, with absolutely no mind of his own, had, during his travels at Uncle Sam's expense, somehow attained the unenviable position of being engaged to three different girls, in three different cities, in three different states. All of whom were madly in love with Big Shark and wrote him at least three times a week, much to his disgust, he being strictly a wolf himself, and a very poor hand at billets-doux besides. Now, ten thousand miles from his nearest fiancée, Big Shark was keeping his exact whereabouts a deep secret, and received no mail at all for months, except one letter from a former wife about some alimony, which he ignored while waxing fat and happy.

Thus we became reconciled to everything but our bread slicer. This vicious contraption, constructed on the general lines of a portable guillotine, was a clumsy affair about as easy to handle as a bulldozer, with a huge wicked blade that was loose and consistently cut an inch farther back than appeared possible. We who were used to precision tools, with electrically operated blades that always cut in the same place, could not, and did not, seem to learn that our bread slicer wasn't to be trusted. It maimed a number of mess orderlies during our stay, neatly slicing a piece out of their fingers and causing them to curse and howl and strike at the thing with their free hand while rich redness splashed into the air and we who were eating discussed the nutritional value of bread soaked in blood.

In a way the bread slicer portrayed quite well the spirit of the whole country. Huge, unwieldy, with a raw brute strength that didn't know and seemingly didn't give a damn for the niceties of civilization as we knew them, this bread slicer (and this country) surged happily ahead in the same old way, totally unaware that it wasn't "streamlined." And we could laugh at it and remark how hopelessly backward it was, but when all was said and done, we were the ones that got our fingers smashed.

ONE DAY some two weeks after we had arrived word came down that thirty-six-hour passes were "authorized." Thirty-six hours of freedom, the stuff we were fighting to maintain but actually saw very little of, loomed up like a two weeks' vacation back in civilian life. Just how this was to be distributed among the personnel wasn't stated, so we worked that out ourselves. Nickel Plate Baker, our first sergeant, wanted to play favorites as usual and bless with freedom those men who might conceivably come home with a bottle of "plonk" and offer him a drink. Spotlight, who happened to be our barracks leader and had recently acquired another stripe, wanted to impress us with his new-found authority and went around roaring, "No pass for you!" on the slightest provocation. We agreed that Spotlight was "stripe-happy" and now and then some hulking private with nothing to lose would tell him so. Eventually, unlike the forefathers of our glorious

Democracy, we decided our freedom with a deck of cards, ace high. Fate smiled; I drew the king of spades and looked around for a pair of 30-33 pants with a press.

At noon next day four of us appeared at the Main Gate shined, pressed, and polished like so many heroes on our way to a Bond Rally. Loftily we offered the M.P. on duty the

passes that stated we were "authorized to be absent from our duties and organization for a period of thirty-six (36) hours" and listed the location of two prophylaxis stations. He gave us the usual fishy stare and admitted there was a train leaving, about one o'clock, he thought. Actually it left at one-thirty-five. We were on it, along with four hundred other soldiers, all shined and pressed as we were, and some, the happy owners of bottles of plonk, rapidly becoming more shined.

The trip to town took two hours. Our train barely struggled up each hill, rolled free down all the grades, and stopped at every station, why we could never figure out. Nobody got on (ours was strictly a G.I. train) and nobody got off, except sometimes a few badly plonked soldiers blearily unaware of just where they were, who got off by mistake, wanted to get on again as soon as the train started and staggered down the various platforms wailing, "Wait! Shtop!" much to the horror of the civilian travelers, who ran mostly

to prim old ladies with market baskets. By American standards our train was inefficient. Rather than signal arms and flashing green lights, orders were passed by word of mouth. When it was time to start, the conductor would swing off the guard car and yell, "Let 'er go, Bill!" or something similar in the general direction of the engineer, who waved airily in reply and "let 'er go." Again, on nearing town, we hauled up at a whistle stop and waited while the station agent, a rather middle-aged lady, called somebody on the phone and talked for several minutes, probably about new babies, we decided. Presently she would come out and inform the conductor, "Central Stition says go on in." He, in turn, would inform Bill, "Central Stition says go on in." Catching the spirit of the thing, we too would all yell, "Central Station says go on in!" Finally, probably in desperation, Bill would toot his whistle and "go on in," the only train, we hoped, on that particular stretch of track.

Sliding through the suburbs we all crowded the windows and hung over the observation platform, waving to an amazing number of small children, whistling at all the girls, and carrying on generally like troops just back from the front. Presently we shot through a long, black, smoky tunnel and jerked to a stop at Central Station. Four hundred soldiers hit the ramp running, as one man, usually before the train stopped, and scattered. Some lucky customers met young ladies and went off with them arm in arm. Other brassy characters tried to meet young ladies obviously waiting for somebody else, explaining at length that this somebody else's outfit "didn't get no passes today," and urging that the best thing the young ladies could do was go off arm in arm with them that had arrived. The rest of us just scattered.

And in the order of their importance discovered that:

The liquor situation was fast becoming acute. Bars or pubs were always attached to a hotel, often hidden away on the second floor, and usually divided into a "Public Bar," a "Private Bar," and a "Lounge." We who were used to the informal atmosphere of Walt's Highway Café confounded no end various proprietors and a good share of the natives by wandering happily from one section to another, caring not a

·damn whether we were "dressed" or accompanied by a young lady. In an effort to square things, of course, we seldom left a lounge without a young lady if we could help it. Many a romance began with the words, "Could I sit down? Could I buy ya a drink?" The answer to both would be a nasal, "Ye-e-ess." The drinks themselves were considerably cheaper and simpler than those at home, the average price being one bob or sixteen cents, and rather than order a "De Luxe Beachcomber" we merely said, "An' bring us a bottle of ginger ale."

But what drinking we did had to be done between the hours of 8 and 10 A.M. (a disgustingly early hour for drinking or anything else), 12 noon and 2 P.M., and four and six in the late afternoon. We who were used to fourteen consecutive hours in which to pub crawl had a hard time becoming accustomed to drinking in two-hour stretches. With the constant threat of "closing time" hanging over our heads we

drank too much, much too fast, and were then turned into the streets where Base M.P.'s with large bulging biceps hauled the too violent off to the clink. While those who weren't violent, only friendly, annoyed all the young ladies who happened to be on the streets between 10 A.M. and noon, 2 and 4 P.M., and after six o'clock.

Later we discovered that most of the smaller bars, particularly those on the outskirts of town, had a backroom or "parlor" reserved for the use of old and faithful friends of the

proprietor. We learned too that with a little diplomacy Yanks who were willing to buy or "shout for" the drinks could often join these exclusive little circles and become partners in the crime of supporting a sly grog shop. While less fortunate Yanks roamed the streets, dodging M.P.'s, and waiting for four o'clock. Generally these old friends were aged characters, originally from England but at pains to convince us they were now Australians and proud of it, full of garrulous tales concerning the "outback in 1900." To a man they had hollow legs, but they were a means to an end.

Sometimes there were young ladies present too. Particularly one hotel that we frequented, The Black Bull—straight out of *Treasure Island*—seemed to cater to the sly grog wants of young married women. One such, a Mrs. McKenzie by name, intrigued me for nearly three weeks, or until I discovered, much to my chagrin, that she was *not* "widowed since Singapore" but the wife of a disgustingly live and near-by foundry worker, a man that she herself described as being "one of them jealous husbands." Rather than meet socially or otherwise the jealous Mr. McKenzie and him probably swinging two ingots of pig iron, I took my business to His Majesty's Royal Hotel and became acquainted with an exceptionally garrulous old character named John, who insisted I come up and meet his sister (eighty-eight) and enjoy a fish supper. The natives were like that, friendly. And mostly they drank socially, for the companionship it offered. The local pub corresponded to our General Store. They didn't sit around a stove on cracker barrels, but they got the same results. We Yanks, of course, went to the pubs and drank because we wanted to get drunk.

When the pubs closed, we went to a dance. In some ways these dances resembled the ones we had known at home. There was music, there was a dance floor, there were girls, there were a couple of mush-faced M.P.'s hanging around looking for trouble. But the actual dancing was something else. Aussies favor dancing around and around with all the dash and originality of a worn-out merry-go-round, repeating in set sequence a series of steps not unlike an old-fashioned Rockette routine. They danced, one after the other, a Two Step, a Quick Step, a Waltz, a Canadian Barn Dance, a Military Waltz, none of them in any way alike. We Yanks

danced regularly too, but we danced a Fox Trot hour after hour and that was the limit of our versatility. And we favored dancing all in one place, having gotten our early training between the tables in various juke joints where floor space was at a premium. The music, too, was far from the Glenn Miller variety of solid swing, always sounding as if the drummer was being worked with a set of strings. Dum-de dum-de dum-de-dum, dum-de dum-de dum-de-dum, and so on far into the night. Through no fault o. the musicians we recognized most of the tunes as ones that had been popular in the States some eight months back. "I Don't Want to Set the World on Fire" was all the rage, and the "Chattanooga Choo Choo" sat derailed four or five times nightly.

After some weeks of argument with the town fathers (who frowned on Sunday dancing), one of our bands—an "American Swing Band"—took over the City Hall each Sunday night and played for a Service Men's dance. This was attended by all the American troops within commuting distance and rapidly degenerated into a brawl. All the repressed jitterbugs lately yanked out of zoot suits picked up a double-jointed WAAF, rolled their pants legs, and "cut a rug." The girls as a rule, being pretty impressed with Yanks anyhow, took to this violent form of exercise with enthusiasm, discarded formal evening wear in favor of slacks (to the utter horror of the town mothers) and learned to cut a pretty decent rug themselves. The male natives preferred to stand well back from the sidelines where they had a chance to survive, and mutter "Thim bloody Yanks dance all over the plice." Nor would they call swing "swing" or "jive." They persisted to the end in referring to it as "Yankee music," or, were they particularly disgusted at the sight of some former young lady acquaintance manfully trying to dislocate her back to the strains of "One O'Clock Jump," they would mutter that our Yankee music sounded like "what the black fellows played."

We tried to explain that our music stemmed from deep in the hearts of the black fellows of our own Southland, but it went over their heads.

In all fairness we tried several of their dances from time to time and found them all something less than exhilarating. Particularly were we discouraged with the Canadian Barn Dance. This little number consisted of everybody circling the floor to the strains of what might have been the "Dead March" from Saul. At fairly irregular intervals the music quavered and broke in a manner that suggested the orchestra had just decided to give the whole thing up. While the leader argued it into resuming, couples joined hands, did a one-two-three-slide movement, followed that with a couple of spins, and, disentangling themselves, the lady moved on and the man turned back, theoretically in time to meet, rhythmically, the lady behind him.

True, this dance had a certain element of surprise. Having finished the required number of spins and twirls with a rather large hefty girl, I would turn to meet my next partner spread-eagled like an all-American tackle, only to find that I was practically overpowering some diminutive four-foot-ten slip of a girl. And finishing with her, I would turn and embrace some tall beanstalk of a girl, gathering her to me just about at the hips, and possibly catching a stinging slap in the face for my error. I noticed too, that the first time around any number of ladies, young and old, met me literally with open arms and a beaming smile, thinking no doubt, "Ha! A handsome Yank!" Usually they started a conversation that ended with a short exclamation of pain, and following a few brief twirls they left, without regret, and feeling, I surmised, like hockey players after a particularly bruising game. The second time around they met me with no enthusiasm whatsoever and kept me, literally, at arm's length. The third time around they broke and ran. I am strictly a Fox Trotter.

The traffic too, like the dancing, caused us a certain amount of trouble. Traveling as it did, by the left, it continually ap-

peared from the wrong side while we were looking the other way. It seemed for a time that our effective strength might be

considerably reduced without our ever seeing any combat, and it was months, really, before we learned which way to look when crossing a street. The only thing that saved us in the

meantime was the general use of charcoal burners as a substitute for petrol. Cars powered with charcoal burners struck several soldiers, but neither party ever suffered anything more serious than being brought to an abrupt stop, charcoal lacking the pep to cause any mortal damage. Several of us decided, however, that rather than return to the States and risk our lives all over again while learning another set of traffic rules, we would just stay in Australia.

The trams we caught on to quite quickly. In fact, being open as they were, on both sides, we caught on to them very quickly indeed, usually on the dead run. This may not have been as safe as the loading plan generally in use by American Yellow Zephyrs, but it was certainly speedier. The fare too, was considerably less, actually tuppence. We Service Men traveled for half fare or a penny, or sometimes, was the conductor particularly war conscious, we traveled for nothing at all. Which impressed us no end.

What impressed us a great deal more was the attitude of the people. While nobody ever actually said so, it was easy to gather that we were generally regarded as the saviors of Australia and very welcome too, considering the ever-growing threat of a Japanese invasion. Better than that was the idea —also generally held, it seemed—that each of us had personally decided to come overseas and do our bit for Australia. After listening to this sort of talk and more talk about what was going to happen to the Japs now that the Aussies *and* the Yanks were here, usually over a glass of spirits, for about a month, we were quite ready to believe it ourselves.

Then there was the way the people treated us. When we'd left the States being a soldier was still two strikes on a guy, and almost every young lady we met figuratively put up her dukes immediately she learned we were in the pay of Uncle Sam. Maybe we were very upstanding young gentlemen, but we were *soldiers*. Now, in Australia, we were soldiers, Yanks, and that was that. It automatically made us very nice guys indeed. Maybe we were actually cads of the first water (and some of us were) but we had to convince our newly made acquaintances of that. They didn't take it for granted.

And we were something new. Glamorous characters from America! The America our friends knew all about from seeing the "pictures." Some of us, the shallow ones, did their best to live up to this advance publicity; some of us did our best to tear it down. Whether or not we succeeded, I can't say. We were the first Yanks to land at this particular Port of Debarkation, and for that reason, horribly new and appreciated. He was a very dull Yank indeed who had any buttons left on his blouse after three trips to town. Some of us took this adoration as only our due. A few of us were embarrassed by it; all of us soaked it up.

Others, I'm afraid, resented it, but they weren't Yanks. They were the A.I.F. Returned. Returned from the Middle

East, after Greece, Crete, Syria, and the Western Desert, they were understandably burned to find the female population gone "Yank crazy." But what could they do? The rest of the population resented highly any slurring remarks about the "saviors of dear old Aussie." So the A.I.F. Returned suffered more or less in silence, got falling-down drunk with that "Devil damn the rest of the world" philosophy that is picked up in the front lines, and tried to even the score by consistently bumming us for all the cigarettes we were fools enough to offer. Now and then they would ask us wistfully, "I s'y,

Yank, d'ya reckon if we went to the Stites the bloody sheilas 'ud go for us like they go for you chaps 'ere?" We told them, "They sure would, Dig." And probably they would at that, women being what they are.

Our uniforms, too, outclassed anything the Australian Imperial Forces could climb into. Compared with these veterans we looked like so many little cadets just out of the local academy and steeped in the tradition that shining brass buttons make a soldier. The A.I.F. ran to sweaters and baggy trousers held up with suspenders, something unheard of in our army. Undeniably they looked like a rough tough bunch of boys, which they were. They'd joined the Army of their own free will, "for the bloody 'ell of it," and gone overseas while the smart lads who considered the A.I.F. a "rough lot" stayed home and played the ponies and waited for the government to "call them up." When this happened, they joined the Australian Military Forces, thus becoming soldiers, at least in name, and nominally in the service of their country, though under no obligation to serve that country overseas where there might be some fighting. This fact allowed that even we Selective Service men could more or less look down on the A.M.F. and refer to them as "Rainbow Soldiers." The A.I.F. continued to look at everybody with a somewhat jaundiced eye and complained bitterly at the lack of plonk.

The newspapers, falling in line with public opinion, carried a daily story (with pictures, on page three) of the happy, smiling American troops and their superior equipment; and on page four a long tirade by the Reverend So-and-So, who regretted deeply the evident increase in "street drinking" and, while not actually coming out and saying so, hinted broadly that troops returned from the Middle East were largely responsible. Which didn't make for good feeling exactly. It was indeed a fairly sad situation. Not that we ever said as much to the young ladies we happened to meet. In the first place they wouldn't have understood, and in the second place, that would have been downright foolish.

Besides, we were never actually mobbed ourselves. And what the ship's stewards had told us about the value of American cigarettes turned out to be something less than true. Our cigarettes were welcome, yes, but the first time I came to town I picked the busiest corner I could find and stood there during the rush hour with a carton of Camels prominently displayed in my left hand. A pickpocket got off with two packages, but that was all. The girls were nice and friendly, but we did *not* have to beat them off with clubs.

The only persons who caused any trouble in that respect were the shoeshine boys. These youngsters went into business immediately they discovered that we Yanks, notoriously well paid, would rather pay two bob for a shine than bend our backs. Within a week of our first pay day little boys infested

all the street corners screaming, "Shine, Yank?" at every passing American, then hanging on his blouse and wailing, "Please, Yank, shine?" then begging, "Well, give us a cigarette, will'ya, Yank?" until—in self-defense—we pushed on muttering, "Just *had* one!"

'05

When approximately twenty-seven hours of our freedom had passed we crawled into one of a variety of establishments (the Hop Inn, for instance, sponsored by the Salvation Army) that offered beds to Service Men at ridiculously low prices. All the beds having been taken long ago, we usually settled for the top of a pool table, and dropped off to sleep.

From which we woke at 7 A.M., not necessarily refreshed, but with an excellent idea of the true significance of that expression "behind the eight ball." We might have slept longer but somebody always wanted to play pool. Once on our feet

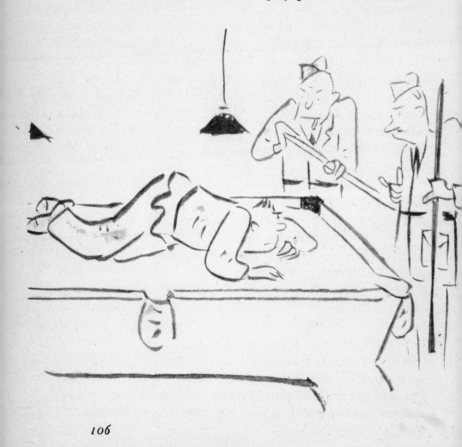

we crept off in the direction of Central Station and waited for the "leave train" that would take us back to camp. Some of us, the confirmed topers, waited in the bar across the street, making a last-minute raid on the "bottle department" that they might be prepared for the trip. I waited in the station restaurant where, being a Service Man, I could drink "real coffee" while probably more deserving civilians struggled along on a variety of substitutes, none of which resembled coffee in the slightest degree.

En route to camp we entertained each other with detailed accounts of the "time" we had had and what we had done with or to who, planned what we would do on our next pass, slept, and drank. Invariably several soldiers became violently ill. Obliging friends would hang them through convenient windows. Somewhat later, on looking at the window and finding it quite empty, these same friends might become fairly ill themselves and spend the rest of the trip worrying about whether George fell out or went some place else on his own hook. They could never be quite sure, as now and then somebody did fall out.

On one memorable trip the conductor, a jolly soul, began accepting the drinks that various soldiers offered him, became as drunk as anybody before we were well out of town, and was of absolutely no value from there on in, refusing even to yell "let 'er go, Bill" at the engineer. When finally we did arrive he wanted to throw up his job (and him with only seven months to go for the pension) and come home to camp with us. It took two brakemen and the fireman to convince him he should stick with the line, and they had to lock him forcibly in the lavatory and threaten to "tell his old lady" before he would listen to them.

Once off the train we negotiated (one way or another) the half mile to camp and slunk past the M.P. at the gate because, chances were, we had broken the 96th Article of War, the

one that says soldiers will not do any of those things that
might be a reflection on or unbecoming to a "member of the
Service." Back in our barracks we took off our "town
clothes," returned those that we had borrowed (explaining
to the various owners how come all the "U.S." buttons were
missing and offering, did these owners get nasty about it, to
give them a couple of addresses so they could go get their
goddamn buttons back) and climbed into our fatigues. Our
thirty-six hours were over. We were ready to maintain freedom rather than enjoy it.

I THINK IT WAS the trip to town that convinced us. Whatever it was, we woke up one morning and opened our eyes and there it was, staring us right in the face, the realization that "this Country is at War." It wasn't the same war we'd known back in the States during those first months of 1942. There weren't many posters and what there were, were mostly faded beyond recognition. There weren't any celebrities out selling bonds; the celebrities were all in England flying Spitfires. Nobody drooled through the radio hinting that Pearl Harbor might never have happened had we all given somebody's soap chips the support they deserved. Nobody went around audibly horrified at the possible effects of gas rationing; that had all happened so long ago the cigarette lighters had a wick instead of a tank. In short, unlike our own country, nobody visibly burst any blood vessels remembering Pearl Harbor or anything else.

They didn't have to. Here in Australia the "bloody war" was old stuff. And did they go to a dance they didn't stand around staring at the national colors in crepe paper or talking to a hat-check girl disguised as the Goddess of Liberty, and thinking "my how patriotic we are." They went to a dance because they wanted to dance and forget the "bloody war" for a couple of hours. When they met each other on the street they made the "V" sign or "thumbs up" and that was about the limit of their demonstrations. But again, they didn't have to demonstrate. The fact that there was a war on became tiresomely self-evident.

And did any of us forget it, we were forcibly reminded immediately we tried to buy anything. The only thing Australia had plenty of was "shortages." There was a shortage of eggs, of most meats, of wood, of clothing, of tobacco, of practically everything else. Gum had disappeared so long ago we didn't even find any stuck to the under side of restaurant booths. Tea, sugar, petrol, matches, all were stringently rationed; civilians being entitled to one inferior box of the latter per week, which is *not* enough for a heavy smoker. Consequently everybody asked everybody else for the loan of a butt, saying, "Give us a light, Mite. Sive the bloody matches." It was quite correct for a young man—even though intoxicated—to offer a lady a cigarette, then lean precariously across the table and offer her a light from his own cigarette. One might easily burn the young lady's face but it "sived the bloody matches."

Actually we Service Men were considerably better off than the rest of the civilian population, that being another big change from the States as we'd last seen them. In most cases, what there was the "Mil'try" got first chance at. This, however, did not apply to clothing other than "issue." If we wanted pajamas we must produce coupons; and we didn't have any coupons. This led to a number of arguments with all manner of clerks, who were invariably polite but firm.

One case in particular I'll never forget, and believe me, I've tried. In town one day, three of us, finding ourselves with nothing to do between "closing time" and "opening time," wandered into a large department store, promptly demoralizing the entire staff. We lurched through the chinaware department, to the horror of the section manager, who could only clasp his hands and pray and hover around in a position to catch us did we altogether lose our balance and start falling through a quantity of glassware. We rode the elevators, completely unnerving four female operators with our lecherous urgings to "stop between the floors." Presently one of us, a former insurance salesman, got lost. The two of us who were left did not bother about him (we found him later, anyway; he'd reverted to type, stumbled into the stockroom, and tried to sell nonexistent policies to a couple of packing boys, age fourteen) and continued riding the elevators until somebody pushed us off on "Lingerie."

A poorer place they couldn't have picked. My companion, an ex-golf pro (his subsequent actions, while probably no reflection on golf pros in general, are nevertheless an interesting phenomenon) immediately decided he must buy his girl a present. Nothing would suit but a pair of pink silk step-ins. Willy-nilly I went along with him. We found sub-department "Step-ins." The clerk, an obviously self-conscious young woman, became quite panicky the moment we hove in sight and made little fluttering movements with her hands, as if to shoo us away. But Al was in no mood to be shooed anywhere. Lurching toward the counter, he said loudly, "I wanna buy a pair of them pants," and that there might be no mistake about what it was he wanted to buy, he pointed a wobbly finger in the general direction of a particularly pink pair of step-ins displayed on the counter.

The clerk, poor girl, became quite pink herself and after a

couple of false starts, managed to gurgle "Do you have any coupons?" Well, no, Al didn't have any coupons, but he brushed that aside as being altogether irrelevant and repeated (louder than before), "I wanna buy a pair of them pink pants." Right about here our clerk, I am sure, would gladly have given us the entire stock and thrown in her own undergarments for good measure. Not being able to manage that, she blushed a deep purple and sidled off like a wounded crab. She was replaced by a decidedly prim old wench who stated quite definitely that unless Al had coupons he was just wasting everyone's time and had better take himself off at once.

But Al insisted. More or less falling over the counter, he picked the step-ins off their rack and held them up for all to see. The old wench tried to clutch them away from him, but Al eluded her and held his treasure even higher. By this time people four or five aisles away were bugging their eyes out, and I felt like the class-play Juliet when her bodice ripped.

Al was apparently oblivious to all this. Falling across the counter again, he breathed alcoholic fumes in the startled face of the clerk and became lewdly confidential. "Look," he hiccupped, "all I want is one pair. They're for my girl. They're jush the kind she likes, see? With elashtic tops." And he vigorously demonstrated the elasticity of this particular pair of step-ins. Whether from the fumes or the horror of it all, I don't know, but the old wench gave up at that and reeled off in the manner of Little Nell on finding she'd "been done wrong." I reeled off about forty feet myself, and stuck my head in a roll of carpet. Two floor walkers appeared, forcibly removed the unmentionable merchandise from Al's hands, and rapidly propelled him out the tradesman's entrance. As far as I know, his girl struggled along on last year's undies and her own coupons.

Had we ever held any doubts regarding the nearness of the war, that experience quelled them.

But there were many other things too, one of the nicest being the advantages offered to "Members of the Services." Having heard about our own "southern hospitality" for some years, then gone South and found public swimming pools discouraging if not actually refusing G.I. bathers, we were mostly pretty soured on this "Serve HIM—HE is Serving You" idea as advanced by various church groups with little or nothing to offer in the way of amusement, and heartily rejected by every establishment that had something to offer but preferred offering it to snappy young civilians and well-paid defense workers. As I say, some of us were pretty soured. Well, Australia kicked that out of us in something less than no time.

For one thing, there just weren't any snappy young civilians. Did we meet any civilians at all, we knew almost to a certainty that they were 4F, mentally deficient, or working twelve hours a day in a war plant and chiefly interested in getting home to bed. More than that, we got the impression that even had the streets been packed with eligible war workers all flush with the first fruits of a job that paid ninety bucks a week, we of the "Mil'try" would still have gotten the choicest service. Not because we were the best customers or the only customers, but because the people just naturally *wanted* to wait on us first. This was particularly noticeable in restaurants, where middle-aged men in pin stripe suits—unless they were an old friend of or "had something on" the proprietor—could darn well sit till they starved or stewed in their own juice, while the waitresses scurried after the wants of various Members of the Services.

The pictures too, operated on the same plan. Only three cinemas were open on Sunday nights (this by special dispensation of the Archbishop, we gathered) and they were reserved exclusively for members of the Services and their guests, one guest per member. The civilian population, unless they knew a Member of the Services, could go for a walk or stay home and play Chinese checkers.

At strategic locations throughout the rest of the town there were scattered a variety of halls, huts, homes, clubs, and lounges, all for the special benefit of Members of the Services, and not one sponsored by the U.S.O. (Which organization, incidentally, we decided had gotten off the boat and gone back to Frisco with the pilot. We'd never seen it or one of its hostesses—the ones that kept getting their pictures in *Life*—in the Southwest Pacific Area.) These halls, huts, clubs, and lounges offered meals for practically nothing as near as we could figure; a limited number of beds and all the floor space they could cover with blankets and soldiers; a place to sit and wait for a friend who never showed up; various sorts of games; a certain amount of female companionship; and usually some kind of a dance.

We frequented all these places, but particularly we liked

the Cheer-Up Huts. There were two of these (called, appropriately enough, Cheer-Up Hut No. 1 and Cheer-Up Hut No. 2), run by some independent organization that cared not a hang for our spiritual well-being and never passed any leaflets or started any hymn-fests, but wanted very much that we have a good time. Practically all the churches sponsored their own huts, but personally I steered clear of them, being naturally leery of entertainment with such a high moral background. Some of the boys smirked it around that they'd met some very immoral characters indeed at the First Presbyterian Hut (which bordered on a factory district) but I stuck to Cheer-Up Hut No. 1.

This hut hugged Central Station and catered almost entirely to Members of the Services. Not all these members were males by any means. There were WAAF's, WRAN's (with, naturally, an overworked gag about "also WRAN's"), AWAS's, AWAL's, WENL's, and a couple of others that sounded like fugitives from our bureaucracy. It would be an interesting fact could I tell what all these outfits were, but I don't know. We cared more for names and addresses than insignia. The "W" always stood for "Women's," and one of the "A's" for "Australian," but that's as far as I ever got. You might truthfully say that I didn't know women from A to Z— but I knew a lot of addresses.

I did gather that the WAAF's were the most numerous and, generally speaking, "good kids"; that the AWAS's "S" stood for "Service"; and the AWAS's, generally, were big brawny girls who (it was rumored) always carried a spanner. The WENL's ("Women's Something Something Something") were the glamour girls of the services. Recruited strictly for their classic profiles and ability to drive, they chauffeured the staff officers of the American Base Section and seldom favored us ordinary soldiers with more than a brief glimpse of their classic profiles going by at twenty

miles an hour with a Base Major (the "Base" is capitalized
and refers to the Major's organization rather than his nature)
hanging over the rear of the front seat. Even at that we
drooled.

It was rather fun finding ourselves comrades in arms with
some of the flower of Australian womanhood, and certainly
novel to think that in case of emergency some five-foot slip
of a lass, a sergeant in the WAAF's, could "pull rank" on us.

We were six months ahead of the bright boys who coined
the same gag when the WAAC's were instituted.

There were other services too, some that we had never even
heard of. The Royal Dutch Navy, for instance, and the A.I.F.,
of course, in strength, and the A.M.F. and the R.A.A.F. and
the R.A.A.N. and now and then a few of His Majesty's Royal

Navy. Our own Navy, or at least a good share of it, we thought, hit town at intervals and rolled through the streets, some in whites, some in blues, and all intensely interested in "where can a guy get a drink in this town after six o'clock." There were Yanks of all descriptions, from all arms and branches of the service, in an amazing variety of "proper uniforms." There were men of the United Nations Merchant Marine, usually in carefully preserved sports suits, who stood around telling each other of their proposed trips on what ships with how many barrels of high-octane gasoline under the deck plates, and promising—did a pig boat blast this loose-lipper and high octane to Kingdom Come—that they who were left would "drop a lei from 'Loo next time we cross the spot."

There were our own Air Corps personnel, Yanks too, of course, but deporting themselves as befitted men who daily risked their lives carrying the war to the enemy. A lot of them didn't really risk their lives carrying the war to the enemy but spent their time standing guard at sundry airports. However, they were careful to keep this fact from becoming generally known and downtown on pass continued to act as men should who saw themselves regularly in all the ads and knew there'd been a song written to the effect that they "Wore a Pair of Silver Wings." A lot of them didn't actually wear a pair of silver wings either, but it didn't bother them; they still knew they were a superior type. They dressed accordingly, in a variety of non-issue "uniforms," with white belts and whistle buttons that would have done credit to an infantry colonel. Now and then one of these glamour boys got picked up by the M.P.'s for "impersonating a second lieutenant."

Finally there were some odd Javanese characters, evidently on our side of the war, but with what service we could never imagine. They stood on street corners leering at young ladies

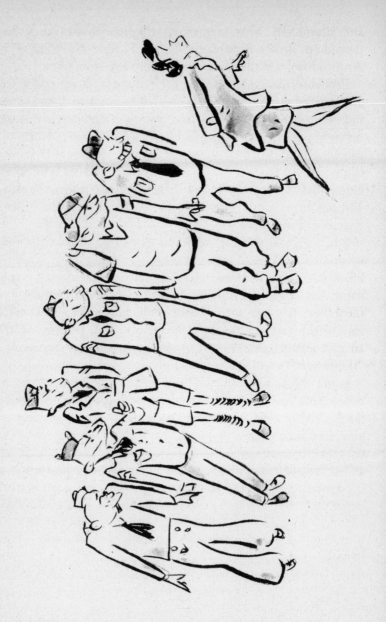

and mumbling what suggestive English phrases they had picked up. Brown or white, in R.A.A.F. blue, Navy white, or Army khaki, we all had approximately the same ideas.

Probably the oddest uniform of all that we ever saw was affected by certain naval individuals (Australian) who slicked their hair and washed their face, polished their boots and put on a visored cap and a shirt and a tie and a blouse and a pair of calf-length socks, then shattered the whole business with a baggy pair of slightly less than knee-length shorts. We knew better, but it was hard to believe they hadn't just come away without their pants. Literally, the whole place looked like a Shriners' Convention.

But, unlike an old Shriners' get-together, it closed up tight at sundown. The black-out, y'know. Officially it wasn't a black-out, only a "brown-out," but whatever it was, it was damn dim. Though rather exciting at first. Stumbling along in the brownness we would watch the blue-white shaft of a searchlight probing through the clouds and, peering at the air-raid shelters, think—with a tight feeling in our stomachs—"this is war."

Later, the brown-out was only a nuisance. And not nearly the help we had imagined when it came to "picking up" young ladies. Young ladies that didn't want to be picked up, wanted even less to be picked up in a brown-out, when they couldn't see what they were getting. Or rather, what was getting them. While young ladies who were willing to be picked up in a brown-out . . . Well, we couldn't see what we were getting either.

WITH THE REALIZATION that "this is a country at war" came a new slant on things. We took a notch in our mental belts. So okay, we were at war. We wrote home to that effect, told our folks all about the real meaning of war, and while we may not have actually mentioned our wonderful spirit of self-sacrifice in so many words, we pointedly implied that what we were suffering was just that. Frankly, it wasn't.

Once we got used to shaving out of a helmet, shaving out of a helmet didn't seem like much of a sacrifice at that. In fact, almost everything, once we got used to it, could be done with a minimum of the spirit of sacrifice. Of course, we never admitted as much, even to ourselves; we only admitted (over and over) that we "could take it" and were certainly tougher and incomparably superior to those troops back home in garrisons where, we remembered, they mopped the floors every day. We mopped our floors not at all. There weren't any mops.

Yes, we bore up wonderfully and lived quite happily with practically none of the comforts of life until presently our fairy godmothers, disguised as the Quartermaster Corps, installed a few comforts of life that left the Diggers assigned to our camp literally slack-jawed with amazement. Foremost of these comforts were our cots, which we took for granted, only complaining bitterly because they were three days late in arriving. The Diggers, on the other hand, hung their chins on their chests and gasped, "Gawd! You chaps 'ave

bloody beds!" Now an Army cot is *not* a Louis XIV canopied four-poster by any means, but we couldn't very well say so when every Digger who saw a Yankee cot reverently tried its resilience and muttered, in an awed voice, "A bloody bonzer stretcher, that's wot she is, Mite."

Some three weeks after our cots appeared it was rumored we had a stove. Personally I didn't actually see any stove for several days, nor did I feel a hell of a lot warmer as I crawled out of bed in the dim gray light of dawn. Still, I was pretty sure we had a stove. Spotlight insisted, almost every night, that I "G'wan out an' get some wood. You aint no better'n anybody else," in a manner that suggested *he* didn't think I was even as good as anybody else. It was while bringing in an armload of wood that I eventually found our stove, smack in the center of a crowd of soldiers that I'd imagined all along as being a crap game.

About as large as a pony of beer, this stove was utterly inadequate as far as heating the wind tunnel we lived in was concerned, but psychologically it was a great help. Often several of us would hover over it, spreading our hands or even opening our shirts, only to find, when somebody took the top off to dispose of his chewing tobacco, that there was no fire. We would immediately clap the top back on and melt away lest Spotlight discover the lack of fire and pack us off to get wood. Usually, shortly before going to bed, we would raid the near-by mess halls, come back with our arms full of anything that we could conceivably heat and eat—heat it, and eat it. Huddled around our red-hot stove we would munch great messy sandwiches of toast and jam and cheese and sardines, discuss (profanely) the non-coms who weren't present, our past and successful encounters with innumerable young ladies, our nebulous futures, the way the war was being run, and anything else anybody happened to bring up. When half the barracks had screamed "Why the hell don't you guys go to bed?" we banked the fire and retired.

And fire or no fire, our stove was a luxury that left the Diggers practically speechless. Possibly they considered it quite unnecessary. All they ever said was, "Jesus! Bloody stoves!" and went on about their business in a drafty sweater and a pair of shorts, all of which made us feel like a bunch of anemics. But warm.

But above everything else that made our lives livable was the Australian version of a service club, the local Red Shield Hut. Run by the Salvation Army, this haven featured a fireplace and hot coffee, and made me wish to heaven I hadn't been so close with my nickels and intent on a double bank every time the Salvation Lassies passed through the pool room back home. I'd like to go on record as saying that our Salvation Army was so far ahead of the U.S.O. when the going got tough that, will it make General Booth any happier,

I'll take coffee instead of a hostess from here on in. And that is a very large statement.

But then it was a large hut. Half of it (the unheated half) was divided into a library and a writing room. The former provided a limited number of books which could be taken out, one at a time, on the honor system, and returned when everybody in the barracks who wanted to read them had read them. The writing room provided paper engraved with a suitable scriptural sentiment and a warning against disclosing anything of a military nature. The remaining half was all "lounge" except a few square feet at one end, partitioned off to form living quarters for the staff, which consisted of a captain who doubled, during services, on the cornet, and a younger man (a cadet, we gathered) who played a heavy hand of organ and led hymns in an echoing baritone. At one end of the lounge was the coffee bar. This oasis dispensed coffee and biscuits (tuppence) milk and biscuits (thrippence) straight biscuits (six for tuppence) and broken biscuits (free) at specified hours during the day and from 7 P.M. until closing. As the coffee was considerably better than any brewed by our own cooks, everybody, with or without an excuse, tried to drop in for a couple of cups during the course of an afternoon. Spotlight, being a naturally vicious character, usually dropped in, too, with a great display of stripes and authority, and dragged off anybody he knew and suspected of being there on "government time."

Opposite the coffee bar, at the far end of the lounge, was a piano and a ping-pong table. There were several incomplete sets of checkers scattered around, and in the middle of the room a small clearing where boisterous spirits might play a noisy game of quoits. There were an electric iron and facilities for pressing clothes, at the other end of a long line of guys, all with three complete wardrobes over their arms and a set expression about the lips that behooved people with nothing but a pair of pants that they had better try again some other week. There was a radio that couldn't be heard when the iron was going, and consequently, wasn't heard.

Halfway between the iron and the piano was the center of all life, the spot we dreamed of from the moment we got up in the morning and crawled into a damp clammy pair of pants—the fireplace. In front of it were perhaps half a dozen battered cane chairs, permanently occupied from the moment we arrived in camp, and behind them some three dozen soldiers waiting to pounce did anybody that was sitting in a chair show the least sign of getting up. Above the fireplace, in large red letters on a white background, was the searing message: "My Strength Is As The Strength Of 10 Because My Heart Is Pure." Day after day and night after night I sat and read and reread those words until I wanted, more than anything else, to smash a coffee cup over some peaceful soldier's head, just to prove I still had a mind of my own. It got so bad I began signing letters "My Strength Is As The Strength Of 10 Because My Heart Is Pure." Which was a fair indication of the shape I was in, but impressed a great deal certain narrow-minded aunts and one particularly narrow-minded and suspicious young lady acquaintance who mostly suspected that I was literally steeped in sin.

Well, I wasn't. In fact, twice a week, every Wednesday and Sunday night, I sang hymns. I didn't have to sing hymns either. Actually there was nothing compulsory about it, but in order to hold my spot by the fireplace I had to stay where the hymns were being sung. Possibly I could have just stayed and sat without participating, but I didn't have the necessary moral (or immoral) strength to sit and mentally view burlesque shows while everybody else stood up and hymned. So I stood with them, and hymned too, after a fashion, and bowed my head (reverently, I hoped) at the right places (I hoped), and kept one foot on the seat of my chair lest some

not so hypocritical soldier tried to steal it. Following the hymns and a short exhortation on the "Right Way of Life" by some imported character who had invariably tried the "Wrong Way" himself but urged that we do without such personal reconnaissance, there were movies (usually an inferior sort of travelogue), and following the movies, free coffee. That, I gathered, being our reward for trying, if only for a little while, the Right Way of Life.

Whether through a desire to get warm or obtain coffee free, or possibly because they wanted to sing hymns, there were always a goodly number of soldiers attending these services. All of whom got beamed on by the captain commanding this particular Salvation Army outpost, and some of whom, at least, must have felt as much a fraud as I did when the recipient of a particularly personal beam. But of one thing we were sure. If we survived, in spite of the "very unusual weather," we could thank the Red Shield Hut and its fireplace, and hot coffee and warmth generally, both physical and spiritual.

As a further aid to our survival we were presently issued winter caps and two more blankets. Most of us had already gone into "longjohns," although I fought against it. Having survived the last six Minnesota winters in nothing heavier than a T-shirt, it was almost a matter of pride. But pride or no pride I got all blue and finally, as a sort of compromise, I put on longjohn tops and both my pairs of pants, fatigue, herring-bone twill. All of which gave me a decidedly lumpy appearance that was nothing to be proud of, but certainly simplified the laundry problem.

As a matter of fact, it soon appeared that we might do something more than survive. We got paid, in Australian money, for two full months, plus what was due us following the raise in pay as finally passed by a Congress we had cursed for five months as a worthless, imbecilic, blubber-headed

bunch of penny-pinching old misers trying to stall our pay raise into an election issue. Plus that twenty per cent for overseas service. All in all a considerable amount of money, seeming more than we had ever received before, it made for a de-

cidedly better pay day than any we had known in the States, where, as a rule, we'd stood in line for nearly an hour and received the something less than munificent sum of seven dollars and twenty cents, that being the only part of our pay we couldn't lay hands on in advance. Probably it was just as well we had so much money coming to us. Otherwise, since nobody, including the Finance Office, was as yet too adept at figuring the rate of exchange, certain avaricious soldiers would undoubtedly have wailed to high heaven about they'd been underpaid. As it was we got a handful of pound notes, about the size that it is popularly believed would "choke a horse," and many of us secretly decided that we had been overpaid. Naturally we said nothing at all about that.

Immediately following this wonderful pay day the American canteen opened its doors, offering to the G.I. public a variety of canned fruits and fruit juices, chocolate cookies, certain inferior kinds of American hard candy, dollar pen-and-pencil sets that sold for "six and two," American cigarettes, and real book matches. Most of this stock we wouldn't have given a second glance (or even a first one) back in the States, but now we gobbled it up just as fast as the canteen personnel could make change. As practically all of this merchandise was labeled "Sea Stores" we bought it tax free, which made a pack of cigarettes sixpence or eight cents in U.S. coin, and impressed us a great deal with the advantages of overseas service. We agreed that it would be a blow when, the war over, we again set foot on U.S. soil and promptly got smacked to the tune of fifteen cents for a package of Camels.

We agreed too, in rare moments of serious talk devoted to something other than "the trouble with this goddamn army," that, coming right down to it, not one of us really wanted to go home until the goddamn war was over.

SPOT OF TEA

WHEN THE FIRST TROOPSHIP full of Americans dropped anchor at a Port of Debarkation every household in Australia put a pot of tea on the fire and sent the younger children posthaste to catch a Yank. We knew of this fact before actually docking ourselves, were all in favor of it, and once landed obligingly went out of our way to help things along. Wandering through the countryside of a Saturday afternoon we would always manage to show up at a particularly inviting home along about three o'clock and moon around, even hanging over the front gate on occasion, until somebody came out, and following the usual palaver about how did we like Australia and really the weather was very unusual, invited us in for a "spot of tea." A "particularly inviting home," in this case, was not necessarily a house with spotless stone steps and well-trimmed hedge, but rather one whose inmates were notably hospitable and included a couple of desirable daughters.

Frankly, the actual "spot of tea" was used by all concerned as little more than an excuse to meet each other. It corresponded, though on a somewhat higher plane, to a jaded American business man's suggesting to his secretary that "we go out and have a bite of lunch together." And it was not the purely social custom where loose-tongued old ladies gathered to thoroughly shred the neighborhood reputations that I had always imagined it to be. Tea was a regularly scheduled meal, served sometime in the late P.M. Just which of our meals it corresponded to we never quite figured out, Australian eating habits, to our way of thinking, being pretty confusing any way we looked at it.

As near as we could ever gather, the first meal in the morning was breakfast. Okay. But the next meal might be dished out about 10 A.M. (which made it "morning tea") or it might be delayed until approximately noon, which made it "lunch" or "dinner," depending on whether it was hot or cold and whether or not there'd been any morning tea that day. The next meal was THE "tea," but was variously referred to as "tea," "a spot of tea," and "afternoon tea." Under special conditions it might even be "supper" or "dinner," depending on whether it was hot or cold, how many meals had already been served, what the last one had been called, and, in some families, who was there to eat it. Shortly before retiring there was still another meal, which the natives usually claimed was supper and we insisted was "just something to eat before going to bed." As we often told them: "All you do all day long is set the table and wash the dishes and wonder what you're going to call it the next time you eat." They told us. "But three meals a day aren't enough! That ruins your stomach." The only thing we were ever sure of was that did we show up at the right gate about 3 P.M. and look sufficiently wistful, we would probably get something to eat, and call it anything we wanted to, it would still be food. We didn't exactly chalk the right gates, as would hoboes of even average intelligence, but we passed the word along.

Our first "spot of tea" was quite an occasion. Five of us, something less than twenty-four hours ashore, were meandering along a back street in the little town nearest our camp. We weren't actually angling for an invitation to tea, though a couple of us had mentioned it as a possibility; we were only hanging around because Al swore he'd seen some girls going into one of the houses. So it came as a bit of a surprise when this pudgy little man appeared on his front porch and said, "Well, what do you think of Austriilia?"

We mumbled one thing or another and he chirped something else and we hung over his hedge like so many starving puppies until he came down off the porch and invited us in to look at his car. Which, being no bigger than a good-sized baby buggy though evidently powered with something (possibly a squirrel on a treadmill) intrigued us a great deal. Our new-found friend explained that the only reason he had a car was that he happened to be a Minister of the Gospel, and anyway, his car was too small to do the government any good. He explained further that he didn't do much driving nowadays, the petrol ration being only four gallons a month. "Four gallons!" we gasped. "Why that would hardly start a car back home!"

And after a couple more gasps all around, the Reverend invited us in to tea. Where we met his rather stringy wife, happily gorged ourselves on a variety of tasty little cakes, discovered that "hot buttered scones" were nothing more than baking-powder biscuits, discussed ad infinitum the States and Australia, and found, when it was all over, that we guests had somehow managed to use less than half the available silverware. Particularly Harold, he who had lost his mess equipment on board ship and survived thereafter with nothing but a spoon, shocked our hosts by using nothing but a spoon throughout the affair, that being the tool with which he had become the handiest.

Luckily this first tea was served on a table, which meant we could lean on our elbows and talk, with gestures, to our heart's content. Most of the subsequent teas we attended were served catch-as-catch-can. Which meant we all sat around on the edges of our chairs (like so many convicted murderers waiting for the jolt of 2000 volts at state expense), balancing our tea on our knees, wondering whether said tea stained a uniform beyond repair, and hoping against hope that the inevitable "accident" and splash and sputtered apologies and dashing after rags to clean up the mess could this time be avoided. As with everything else, there was a shortage of chinaware, and a really serious accident (say two cups and a saucer) would go a long way toward pruning a budding friendship.

Some of us tried to solve the problem by installing small flat boards in our pants legs, just above the knees, but it made for a very odd sort of walk. I heartily disliked catch-as-catch-can teas because, being a guy who can't talk without gestures, I necessarily remained stupidly silent with both hands clutching my cup at all times. Which led people to think "what a dull boy he is" and pass me by when handing out invitations to "come again." Eventually, of course, I mastered some of the elementary aspects of juggling and no longer had to refuse a second piece of anything merely because I didn't know how I could manage it. I caught up on my conversation too, often

gesturing airily with a large piece of insufficiently mortared sponge cake and literally scattering crumbs to my audience. All well-nigh invaluable training for any literary teas that I may ever attend.

As a flying start on a career of teaing we set out that first day to talk an arm off and bore beyond words our Reverend host and his stringy wife. We told them of our adventures in convoy on the high seas, how we suffered aboard ship, how stifling the weather had been, how we had literally come through it all by the skin of our teeth, being a bare one thousand miles away from the Coral Sea Battle shortly after it was all over. We spread it around quite some that we had indeed had experiences, and undoubtedly impressed the Reverend with our willingness to share them. When we had talked ourselves into a state of exhaustion he casually mentioned that he had been in Rabaul when the Japs landed there. Escaping inland with three other missionaries, he'd crossed the island on foot, fought his way south in an open boat, the target of half the Japanese Air Force, eventually reached Milne Bay, and been evacuated from there to Australia; where he was happily tending another flock and slowly regaining the thirty-five pounds he'd lost. The Reverend told this much as we would have explained our whereabouts of the night before had we come in exceptionally late and aroused the family suspicions —apologetically, fluffing over the high spots. He said his wife had been much luckier; she'd left Rabaul on the last boat and suffered nothing worse than two bombings all the way to Townsville.

We thought of what we'd suffered. A shortage of Coca-Cola and no female companionship. On the way home we agreed that what we'd often heard was true—Americans talk too much.

Not that we shut up; we merely agreed that it was true and went right on talking. We didn't like mutton and we said so, over and over. The natives couldn't understand this as a rule, but one Australian war correspondent, visiting us for a few days, notched himself a small niche in the Hall of Something or other by dispatching a masterpiece of understatement to the effect that "we had not learned to relish mutton to any great extent but still preferred beef." To any great extent, hell! Given a choice we would have preferred our war correspondent, who *was* rather chubby.

Of course, we only got mutton once a week—on Thursdays. On Saturdays it was pork, on Sundays, ham. We learned to tell what day it was by the appearance of our mess kits. So mostly we complained about the quality of beef. During a protracted potato shortage, we got macaroni and complained bitterly about that. When the shortage eased off we complained about the size of the potatoes. We stated, emphatically, that the food wasn't like the food "back in the States." Well, it wasn't. And at first the natives, on hearing such statements, only muttered in their beer about the "bloody war" and remarked that *they* had gotten to the point where they were substituting rice for macaroni. Later, when it appeared that we weren't actually out staving off a Japanese invasion, but were, in fact, possibly more interested in certain little invasions all our own, the natives became more straightforward about the whole matter. Following Thanksgiving we were forced to admit that we'd had "a real meal, with turkey an' dressing an' everything," and we inquired of our civilian friends, "What'd you have?"

"Ham," they told us. "You Yanks got all the turkey."

Following Christmas we were again forced to admit that we'd had "a real meal, with cranberry sauce an' fruit salad an' all the turkey I could eat"; and we inquired again of our civilian friends, "What'd you have?"

"Ham," they told us. "You goddamn Yanks got all the bloody turkey!"

Following New Year's we kept out of sight.

We learned too, that discussing any of the large breakfasts we might have had was not a wise move. For, did we casually remark, "Had a purty good breakfas' this morning, got five eggs myself," our friends would gasp: "Five! We ask the bloody shop for six and they give us one!" Just what a family could do with one egg we never had the nerve to ask. As a matter of fact, we seldom had the chance, our friends usually continuing, in a loud wail, "You goddamn Yanks get *everything!*"

Strictly speaking, that wasn't true. Some things couldn't be had. Nowhere did we ever find anything that compared with the American White Castle System, the nearest approach to our twenty-four-hour wonders being various milk bars serving a limp sort of milk shake that always tasted like discouraged vanilla, no matter what they called it. But the milk bars all closed up tighter than a fruit-jar cover at 11 P.M. As did everything else except the M.P. station and here and there a "pie shop." Since practically nobody ever went to the local Gestapo headquarters of his own free will, these pie shops were always crowded to overflowing. The overflow stood

around in the alleys cursing the Blue Law attitude that forced everybody home to bed before midnight.

I never did get inside one of these pie shops. Once, during a particularly black brown-out, two of us saw a door closing in somebody's face and rushed up in time to tap this character on the chest. "Hey, Bud," we asked him, "wouldn't they let cha in?" "No!" he grunted and stumped off, the silver leaves that made him a lieutenant colonel and an officer and a gentleman by Act of God and Congress winking in the dim light. Appalled but heartened at our own boldness, we tried to argue with the guy who was closing the door in people's faces. He wouldn't let us in either, but he told us what they had to offer in the way of food. Pies, fruit or meat, fish and chips, and coffee. It didn't sound too appetizing.

What we could buy came very reasonable indeed. The "austerity" prevented anyone from spending more than five shillings or eighty cents on a single meal and frowned on soldiers who tried to eat two meals at a single sitting. Anyway, in order to spend five shillings we had to frequent places that went in for reserved tables and snowy tablecloths and considerably more silverware than was really necessary. Ordinarily a meal—a "good" meal—cost around three and six, a price so low we refrained from stealing any of the unnecessary silverware.

The American canteen served what were enthusiastically advertised as "Real American Hamburgers" and eventually certain sharp operators around the town alleged that they were selling "Real American Hamburgers" too, but neither institution quite made the grade. Most of the operators being just a little too sharp, they tried to slip a certain percentage of mutton between their buns. A cruel blow to international friendship, it left us appreciating, for the first time, the real meaning of "100% PURE HAMBURGER," as advertised by the American quick lunch.

In the end we readily admitted something we had never so much as dreamed of back in the States—camp chow was better than town chow. Much better.

NORTH TO THE SUNSHINE

LIKE ALL TROOP MOVEMENTS, our particular troop movement was preceded by a solid month of rumor mongering.
As soldiers we were supposed to know the dangers of a loose
lip, and we agreed that the civilian population should be kept
in the dark regarding our proposed whereabouts. But among
ourselves we loosened lips like a bunch of Ubangis learning
"Peter Piper picked a peck of." We were going to India,
China, New Caledonia, Port Moresby, Darwin, Perth. Even
the decidedly ugly rumor that we were going back to the
States and reorganize made its first appearance. In short, as
usual, we were going every place anybody knew the name
of, as long as it was North. After two winters in a row we
were pretty sold on the land of perpetual summer and went
around screaming, "North! North! North to the sunshine!"

Possibly we screamed too loud, or maybe we hinted too
broadly, or perhaps they had other sources of information;

but whatever it was, the civilians round about were never at all in the dark concerning our plans. As a matter of fact, they knew a hell of a lot more about the whole business than we did. It was discouraging. We tried, naturally, to impress various young ladies with guarded remarks concerning our imminent departure, this time for "The Front." "Yep," we told them, "I guess this is the last time I'll ever see this town. And maybe it's the last time I'll ever see you, Honey!"

"Shoo!" they told us. "You'll be in again. You ain't leaving for a fortnight yet. I know. My old man works for the rileway." Often they went on to tell us where we were going (within a hundred yards), how long it would take, what route we would travel, what we would see along the way, and how we would like it after we got there. One young lady gave me this rigmarole three times and accused me, the fourth time, of being a boy who cried "Wolf!" (She accused me of *being* a wolf, too, but that's another story.)

Anyway, she was right (about our departure, I mean). We didn't leave immediately. We hung around for nearly three weeks, got ourselves alerted twice with no sign of a troop movement, turned in our winter caps and overshoes (and what a happy day *that* was), drew mosquito bars, listened to sundry lectures on sundry poisonous insects we might expect to encounter, and mongered more rumors until it was generally agreed that rather than "serve in silence" we should always repeat what we heard and rapidly drive stark raving crazy all the enemy agents who might be tapping us for reliable information. Our C.O., a sensible man, suggested that rather than talk so much we would do well to get rid of the stuff we didn't need and devote some energy to laying in a supply of cookies or something. He had heard that en route we would eat at Australian camps and "you know what that means."

We certainly did. With visions of water tanks full of mutton stew staring us in the face, we got down to business and religiously stole everything edible we could lay hands on. We cleaned the canteen out of tinned fruit and chocolate cookies, then went to work on the mess hall. We stole bread and butter, cream cheese, jam; Sergeant Rubitkish, through a masterful bit of scheming, smuggled four six-pound cans of high-grade pork sandwich meat out of the Officers' Mess. Al, on K.P. for the day, slipped off with two dozen eggs, hid them under his pillow, and slept on his hands and knees for a week lest he break them. Feeling, he said, not unlike a sitting hen in the meantime. Izzy Popopliss (a World War I veteran, Izzy had divorced his wife following Pearl Harbor, picked up an extra set of false teeth, and promptly enlisted in the United States Army. He had insisted on coming overseas with us in spite of his age, and now, at forty-one, called himself "the oldest Pfc. in the goddamn Army." We called him "pop" and "old man," but were glad to have him around. At forty-one he knew *all* the angles.) . . . he contacted a friend who was deep in the black market and came home with eight pounds of tea.

When none of us could conveniently carry what we had stolen, Tex and I consolidated with Izzy and Al and Sergeant Rubitkish. On the assumption that a couple of barracks bags more or less wouldn't be as noticeable as half a dozen boxes all spouting stolen property, Tex and I crammed our belongings into his barracks bag that we might fill mine with what didn't belong to us in the way of Class I supplies. At the last minute Nickel Plate Baker, the first sergeant, showed up with a wheel of cheese and a sack of oranges, and announced that he had decided to join our little group too. We weren't exactly in favor of this, knowing damn well that Nickel Plate, a notoriously hearty eater, desired to travel with us, not for our companionship but for our food. His presence, however, did add a certain amount of prestige and, we pri-

vates thought, might excuse us from certain nasty details that were bound to arise, this Army being the way it is about "leaving a place as clean as you found it."

As a matter of practice, immediately most of the company had gone we who remained behind spent two whole days in a mammoth scrub-fest that left three of our four barracks a great deal cleaner than we had found them. That accom-

plished, we all moved into the fourth hut and sat down to wait for a train. While we waited various characters dropped in and gradually stripped us of the things that made life livable. Some fiends from the QM dismantled and removed our stoves; a Digger lancejack informed us it was time we turned in our straw ticks; somebody else came by and appropriated our cots. Finally a detail came through and picked up our extra blankets. Supposedly, they took two from each man; actually, several men who were absent at the time lost up to four blankets apiece and slept even colder than the rest of us for the next few nights. When it was all over we sat around like a family that had just had a peculiarly unsuccessful brush with the finance company and discussed the possibilities of our train's ever showing up. Originally we had heard it would arrive Saturday P.M., then it was alleged as due Sunday evening, then "sometime" Monday, then Tuesday at eleven, then Tuesday late in the afternoon, then early Wednesday morning. Which was bad enough, but what was worse, our mess, in the meantime, steadily deteriorated. First the butter disappeared, then the jam, then the sugar; presently there was nothing left but corn flakes, very dry and very crunchy. Somebody, we decided, was cutting things too goddamn fine. Not that we suffered; we dug into the stuff we had stolen against just such an emergency, or snided-off to town in the afternoon and gorged ourselves on ham and eggs. Left to his devices the American dogface seldom suffers acutely.

Late Thursday P.M. our lone remaining officer stuck his head in the door and said, "Okay, men, pack up. We'll load at eight o'clock." We packed, wondering again at the amazing amount of trash and trivia a soldier can accumulate in the space of a few short weeks. Al being in town saying good-by to his girl for the umpteenth time, Tex and I packed his stuff too. Al was never properly appreciative of this good turn. On returning (some sixth sense led him back to camp several hours earlier than usual, a scant forty-five minutes before we departed bag and baggage) he discovered that somehow in the hustle and bustle Tex and I had carefully packed all our own clothes and were wearing *his* best pants. Willy-

nilly, being separated from all our baggage that wasn't edible, we wore Al's pants throughout the trip, utterly destroying the press and spilling several pots of jam on them besides. Al swore at us for days, except when he wanted to borrow our toilet articles. (We had inadvertently packed his away where they couldn't be reached.)

Except for this trouble with Al everything went off smoothly enough. We loaded into trucks at around nine o'clock, were convoyed through the darkness to God knows where, and unloaded at the usual blacked-out freight yard. Our train, we learned, would be several hours late. Frankly, this fact was not entirely unexpected. We took off our packs, raided a near-by fence for fuel, and built a fire in the ditch. Having eaten nothing for nearly four hours, we dug out some groceries and had toasted ham and egg and cheese sandwiches and the first of Nickel Plate's oranges.

That night was one of the first occasions when what is generally referred to as the "comradeship of arms" was something you could almost reach out and wrap your fingers around. In the darkness it was impossible to pick out the soldiers that, for some reason, I didn't like. It was impossible to distinguish one squad or platoon or company from another and think "there go them stinkers from 'H' Co." Rather, there were just a bunch of guys in the blackness, something bigger than the Company or the Regiment or even the Army. Just a bunch of guys, from here and there, plopped down on this particular night, in a strange place, ten thousand miles from home. We had no more than a vague idea of where we were and an even sketchier idea as to where we were going. Whether or not our folks or higher headquarters or anybody else knew or cared where we were or where we were going seemed highly questionable. We got the idea

that at least for the time being we were pretty much on our own resources, just another bundle of chaff in the threshing machine of war. Instinctively, alone in the night, we leaned on each other; and resourcefully enough, tore down the fences and built fires. Each fire became separate, surrounded by a little group of men who swore at but considered each other as "friends," and thought "this here is the *damnedest* bunch of guys in the world." And looking at all the fires we felt—more than that, we knew—that did the need arise these men would turn on the rest of the world for each other.

Our train arrived at two-thirty. We clambered aboard in the darkness—our little group, with Nickel Plate's authority, grabbing an end compartment and refusing to let anybody else in. I'd come halfway around the world at this point and, from the way our train was pointing, it appeared that I was starting back. So far it had all looked disgustingly alike— and that disgustingly like a blacked-out freight yard at three in the morning. It looked somewhat better when we at last got under way and skimmed (if it is possible to "skim" at twenty-five miles per hour) along through the open country-side. Presently we settled down to sleep out what nobody expected to be a particularly comfortable night. Nobody was disappointed.

After flipping several coins and arguing for some time about "Awchrist, no! It's gotta be two outa three," I ended up with a length of hard leather seat that would have cramped a dwarf. (I am five-foot ten in my stocking feet and I sleep with my shoes on.) Still I fared better than Izzy and a character named Whitey, who, having lost the toss and the argument, shared a similar seat just across the aisle and sat up all night glowering at my relative comfort. I slept some between stops that drove my head through the end of our compartment, and woke at 5 A.M. to find Whitey slumped on the floor and Izzy huddled in his overcoat, with his

gloves and overshoes on, a raincoat wrapped around his legs, and his overseas cap pulled down about his ears. He looked like Napoleon's retreat from Moscow, Third Class, Non-smoking.

Thus we rolled north to the sunshine, much as our ancestors had rolled west to the Golden Gate by ox cart, and at approximately the same speed. Our train was composed of reconditioned rolling stock on loan, I think, from the National Museum. It was "second class." That is, the compartments were only partially enclosed, and any soldier who had the nerve to break up four poker games, wake half a dozen customers asleep with their feet across the aisle, step on a couple of others asleep in the aisle, and spill several checker games, might wade the length of the car. There were more such nervy soldiers than you might think. And as luck would have it, our group had grabbed an end compartment

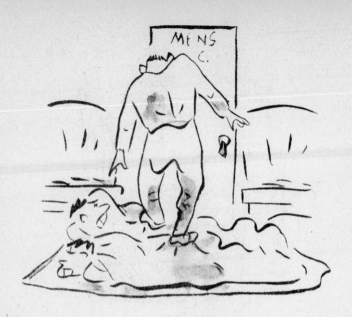

before ascertaining the location of the door marked "Men's Water Closet." Said door was at our end. Day and night for ninety-six hours a variety of strange clumsy soldiers bumped and smashed their way through our home in search of this door. We longed for the comparative luxury of a "first class" carriage, where each compartment had its own water closet, and offered as much privacy as could be expected considering the acute shortage of rolling stock.

At times five soldiers in the same compartment, be it first class or second, can be several too many. Each night we tried a different sleeping arrangement, none of which proved too successful. By pooling our blankets and shelter halves, three of us found we might have slept quite comfortably on the floor had it not been for the club-footed bastards who stumbled through at odd hours and stepped all over us while looking for that door. Later, I tried to sling a hammock, us-

ing my shelter half and a couple of convenient baggage racks. Three nights in a row Tex, a pessimistic soul, warned me: "She'll never hold, Jack." Three nights in a row he was right. And while it made him less pessimistic (happy even) to watch me crashing to the floor like a dead ripe tomato, Al, who slept beneath me and aided a great deal in breaking the fall, was never at all impressed with the humorous aspects of the situation. When there were only four of us in a first-class smoking compartment, we worked out a complicated system that entailed redistribution of all the movable seat cushions but provided fairly satisfactory beds. The only disadvantage being Harold, who refused to sleep backwards (with his head in the direction we were going) but could sleep no other way without putting his head in the water closet, which he didn't favor either, and complained bitterly each night because nobody would trade beds with him.

En route some of us passed the time playing cards or checkers. Others merely crouched at the windows, waiting for the next girl to wave at. All of us traced our daily prog-

ress on small maps we found glued to the walls of our compartments, originally for passengers who had been chiefly concerned with the scenic spots of interest to be found along the way. *We* were chiefly concerned, each morning, with what, if any, we had gained during the night, and never failed to shout, "How far to the nex' town?" at any natives we happened to find along the track. Mostly these natives didn't answer anything worth while, but contented themselves with looking amazed and making "thumbs up" or "V for Victory." Which, while cheering, didn't increase our knowledge of the terrain worth a damn.

Now and then one of us would take his life in his hands and attempt a shave while the engineer played crack-the-whip and hunted out particularly long black sudden tunnels to roar through. We could, of course, have shaved while at one of the stations where our train stopped (probably for a general overhauling, we thought) but the time spent at such stations was all too precious to waste shaving.

Usually we stopped three or four times a day, but no matter where or when or how often we stopped, when we did, we ate. Some days we ate twice, most days we ate three times, and on one memorable day, for no apparent reason, we ate no less than six times. Not at Australian camps, either, as our C.O. had feared, but right at the stations. The food was prepared by a variety of Women's Volunteer Groups, and while it ran to fat pudgy bright-red mutton sausages, it was still much better than we had expected. Some places served a tastier lunch than others, and most of us, when later discussing the trip with friends who had come on a different train, referred to towns, not by name, but as "that place where they gave us cocoa." Certain whistle stops with practically nothing to offer in the way of municipal advantages still loom large in our memories because they gave us "seconds."

Naturally it didn't take us long to catch on to this eating deal. Did somebody say, "Hey! We're coming to a town!" everybody grabbed his mess kit and hung far out the nearest window in direct violation of an order that said "Heads or limbs will not protrude through car windows." Immediately

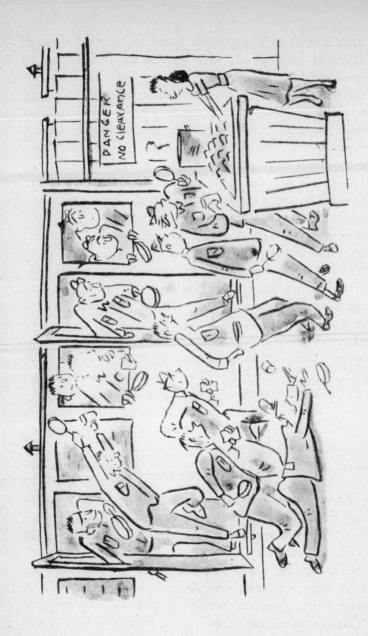

the train slowed to a reasonable speed we hurtled through the doors, lit running, and kept on running to the spot we presumed would be the head of the chow line. Or most of us did anyway. Certain individuals, of course, lit running, eluded the slow-witted guards posted to prevent just this sort of thing, and scattered in search of the nearest pub. On returning they were met at the station gate by an officer, who relieved them of any bottles they happened to be carrying or concealing, and ordered them back to their respective compartments. The bottles disappeared into the train commander's car, which, on our arrival, could have been (and should have been, some claimed) sidetracked and set up in business as one of the best-stocked bars in all Australia.

Other soldiers concentrated on what female companionship these various stations offered. The way it worked out, what girls could be found, could be found with their backs to a wall, surrounded by half a hundred such drooling soldiers, all talking at once, and firmly convinced that they, personally, were making a BIG impression. Some of these one-horse Gables hinted they'd gotten past the conversational stage with a couple of the girls who met the troop trains, but probably they were just carried away by the general feeling, a feeling that led the local belles to say, when they said anything, "Oh! You Yanks!" Other two-cylinder Boyers, laboring under the mistaken impression that they were "irresistible," would insist, following a brief twenty-minute acquaintance, that all concerned kiss each other a fond farewell before our train pulled out and carried us off to "The Front." Very few were in any way as irresistible—or successful—as they had imagined they would be.

When we did get under way everybody hung through the windows again, screaming and waving good-by. Not once, at this stage of the game, did we miss singing a solid version of the "Chattanooga Choo Choo." And until you have heard five hundred male voices raised in a raucous rendition of "Pardon me bo-o-o-oy," accompanied by a gasping locomotive, and interspersed with shrill whistles as we swept by some particularly juicy bit of Australian pulchritude, you haven't heard anything. Literally, we went north to a boogie beat.

Always, too, as we were leaving, certain soldiers who had delayed too long with one of the girls who happened to be around came dashing down the platform frantically searching for their compartment and, were they unable to find it, leaped aboard at the last possible moment and crowded into any old compartment, much to the disgust of the rightful occupants. Later, unless these late comers ran into some old friends, they would usually attempt a hazardous trip back to their own compartments, using a narrow guard walk that ran along the sides of the carriages and any convenient windows they could hang onto, always hoping that nobody would open a door and brush them off into space. All this to the utter horror of our train commander, a major who figured his chances of a lieutenant colonelcy would be better if he arrived without any men "Missing, Lost in Transit."

He need not have worried really. At least six of us were in much better physical condition when we arrived than when we left. Having little to do but eat and watch the countryside, we did just that. And thanks to our being somewhat too enthusiastic about laying in a supply of stolen food for the trip, we had, as Sergeant Rubitkish put it, "More goddamn garbage than six hogs could eat." Actually we had around 180 pounds, which figured out to a little better than seven pounds per man per day, or four pounds more than we could comfortably consume. We ate steadily, all day long, and anybody that refused anything was considered a downright saboteur. We gave stuff away, some to other less fortunate or well-prepared soldiers, or now and then, when we stopped far out in the country for a "latrine call," we sent the small children who invariably showed up uninvited at these affairs staggering home under the weight of everything we could press upon them. Nickel Plate's wheel of cheese haunted us, becoming grimier and smellier and less appetizing with each passing day, until, in desperation, we dropped it out the window while crossing a particularly high trestle.

Military Secrecy prevents mention of how many times we "changed gauge." Suffice to say that had we changed once more we fully expected a single rail and travel in coaches no wider than a small yawn. As it was we rocketed precariously along the last few miles, sitting quite carefully lest we upset

our train. Nothing (such as brown-skinned little wenches that the natives called "blacks" or "Aboes" and we called "Abies" or—if we were educated—"mulattoes") appearing that might cause a mad rush to the windows, we presently again arrived safely at a destination and detrained, wonder of wonders, at three o'clock in the afternoon. We whispered it around that somebody would certainly get chewed for letting us arrive any place in the daytime, and agreed that in this case it might have been just as well for all concerned had we arrived in the dead of a very black night. Our destination, at first glance, appeared something less than intriguing.

It was flat, hot, dry, and dusty, with here and there a few palm trees that we might eye suspiciously. The regimental band had turned out to greet us, blowing their collective brains through a variety of horns. We jeered at them and screamed they should turn that junk in for salvage. Nevertheless, we were glad they had come. The Glory of War, as portrayed by martial music, rolling drums, and piping fifes, is so much applejack; but just plain war, without any piping fifes at all, would be a much tougher proposition.

The guys who had arrived previous to us were there too, and they, in turn, jeered at us who had probably had a real bath within the past two weeks. We told them they were "bivouacy" and inquired about the liquor situation. They laughed harshly at that, implied we were just plenty damn naïve, and pointed to a lone weather-beaten hotel that advertised the familiar "XXXX Bulimba Beer." "That," they told us, "is it. But it ain't had no beer since Tuesday."

The reunion over, we loaded into trucks, and rumbled off. Presently we entered a woods and wound down narrow twisting roads, meeting at every corner a plunging six-by-six truck with a maniac at the wheel. Eventually we came to a sign "Hq Co" and turned into what appeared impassable jungle. The trucks stopped, we unloaded. Somebody pointed and said, "Your tent is over there, about a hundred yards. Don't get lost, an' hurry back. We're messin' with 'M' Company."

We were "home" again. We were north. North to the Sunshine! Now and then a small patch of said sunshine filtered through the foliage. "Well," said Tex, "anyway, she's dry."

One of the old boys said, "Haw! Dry, hell! The rains are coming. In about two months, a guy told us. An' when it rains here, it rains for two months, every goddamn day!"

It seemed reasonable enough. The next time we moved, we were going to India. For the Monsoon.

THE FIRST TIME we stood retreat at our new home the C.O. informed us that what we were now in was a "staging area." He implied, without actually saying so, that this knowledge should imbue us with a proper spirit of resolution and a love of rigid training. All work and no play makes Jack a tough soldier. Usually it makes him mad at the whole world too, which is the right attitude.

In the weeks that followed, our C.O. read for our benefit various communications from the regimental commander, the divisional commander, even the Commander-in-Chief. Addressed to "all personnel" or "troops of my command," these communications reaffirmed our presence in a staging area and stressed in stilted language the extreme desirability of physical fitness and mental alertness on the part of all, officers and men alike; and suggested that in view of the drastically reduced pass privileges, we wallow in the joys of "rigid training." Read to our particular bunch of personnel immediately following various Retreats, these communications did not noticeably impress anybody, but merely delayed Nickel Plate's brief appearance with a few words on how our tents all looked like "boars' nests" again. These over, Nickle Plate dismissed us, allowing we might scatter to our boars' nests for a short rest until chow time and some discussion of the various young women with whom we had had or almost had or would certainly liked to have had an intimate acquaintance in the past. The song was ended, but the melody lingered on.

Though not without a struggle. Training was indeed rigid. The old Army tradition, Wednesday and Saturday afternoons off, did not, it seemed, hold good in a staging area. They, instead, were given over to "organized athletics," which, while possibly a form of recreation synonymous with

"time off," entailed a two-mile hike to the nearest piece of open ground that would accommodate a company doing anything more extended than lock-step dancing. Lectures were cut to a minimum; rather than become confused by listening, we learned by doing. Most of our transportation being grounded in the interests of one thing or another, this doing meant a great deal of hiking. As a matter of fact, we hiked every day, which is indeed a great deal, learning to knock off with a fair degree of nonchalance fifteen miles per every five hours, and working out, in the meantime, some decidedly cynical little gags regarding our supposedly "motorized" regiment. A fair sample being: "Don't worry about it, Jack. Just recap my goddamn knees and I'll make 'er." As the dusty weeks marched by at a steady cadence of 120, we agreed that perhaps a little rain might not be so bad at that, did it bring us a few hours of "bunk fatigue." And we learned to look forward to Sunday, which was still a day of rest.

Later, when we were lean and hard, we went on a long hike that corresponded, in our case, to the summer camp following four years of R.O.T.C. Not that our post-grad work resembled in any way an R.O.T.C. fiesta. We carried full field equipment—an outfit that includes everything a soldier owns except his Service Record. At the end of the first hundred yards Harold, who had wangled himself a driver's license and spent the last month flat on his back under an oil pan, groaned "Oooooh!" and cursed heartily the unknown Plans and Training officer who had first thought of such a hike. Harold repeated this performance every hour on the hour for two days while we plugged steadily southward along ever narrowing and decidedly unimproved roads. Arriving at a spot so far from civilization the towns were called "stations," we left the road (a few minutes, I think, before it was due to leave us) and struck off into the "bush," supposedly uninhabited country that the natives referred to as "rough" and we called "One goddamn hill after another." Actually this country was not entirely uninhabited, nor were we exactly the first white men to lay eyes on it. Now and then, far back in the bush, we came across a customer tying corn to the side of a hill that, back home, would have been used strictly for motorcycle contests. These gentry were invariably quite cheerful and asked us (naturally) what did we think of Australia? At the time, with Australia rising all around us to a height of what must have been several thousand feet, we who were frank but decent said nothing; while we who were only frank left numerous farmers with a decidedly shaken opinion of their homeland.

One night we stopped near a house. Two of us went to the door with a carefully prepared story supposed to explain our presence in the vicinity, intending to ask if we might buy some milk. We were somewhat surprised when the woman who opened the door, giving us no more than a glance, called, "Oh Ma-a-arge, bring the milk. They's more Yanks here." Marge, on investigation, confirmed our suspicions. Asked to come down and see our bivouac, she squirmed and smirked and murmured, "No-o-o, she didn't reckon she'd better. They'd been some Yanks here before. . . ."

We learned to look for signs of these other Yanks, and watched carefully for long streamers of toilet paper hanging from some prominent tree. Which, while possibly not in the best woodcraft tradition, were certainly a hell of a lot easier to spot than a pile of stones. We watched too for empty "C" ration cans left lying around by former companies, but gave *them* as wide a berth as possible because sometimes our officers made us bury the darn things. Now and then we came across an empty bottle of shaving lotion, dropped by some

soldier who had found—as we did—that it was a peculiarly unnecessary article in the "bush," serving only to attract flies. We learned that rather than hack our own trail we had only to stand around looking lost and presently a dirty little boy would come running across the fields screaming, "Yu wanna find the path, Yank?"

Thanks to numerous such little boys, we eventually came out of the bush, found the rest of the company, and bivouacked, fully convinced that we were quite exhausted. Until word got around that there was a "right town" less than eighteen miles distant. A bottle of beer and a girl, or promise of same, having much the same effect as adrenalin, a good many of us decided we weren't so exhausted after all and set out to find this town. Two of us found it and a bottle of beer and what—under the circumstances—passed for companionship, and returned to our bivouac area by taxi for a fare slightly less than the original cost of the vehicle. As American soldiers we may have had more money than any of the rest of the world's G.I.'s, but that was through no fault of the local cabbies.

Tumbling into bed I got roundly cursed by Al, who happened to be sleeping in the middle that night and was highly incensed to think that I should deprive him of fifty per cent of his warmth until 4 A.M. Up at six, he cursed me again for falling asleep in the middle of my first cursing. We climbed a mountain, met some trucks, and rode back to camp, Al cursing me at intervals all day long, whenever he thought of the dastardly thing I had done to him. He has never really forgiven me.

Though few of us ever admitted as much, we did learn several things of value from our hike. Personally I discovered that hills cannot be climbed day after day in the manner of a minor clerk dashing six flights to beat the time clock. To coin a phrase, slow but steady wins the race, and them that are called Rabbit Ears will probably peter out on the first ridge. All of us, I think, became convinced that until the kitchenware genius who invented the mechanical potato peeler comes up with a somewhat similar, collapsible, and preferably soot-proof business in which to heat the Army "C" ration, the Army "C" ration will best be eaten cold, direct from the can. Heating the "C" ration involves a certain amount of trouble, mostly explained by the old Ojibway saying: "Indian build little fire, sit close; White Man build big fire, keep warm hauling wood."

On the other hand : "Indian wear woolly underwear; White Man, if sleep warm, must build one helluva big fire." As a matter of training we were supposed to get along with a minimum of fires. Many were the substitutions hopefully introduced, not one of which proved very successful. Several soldiers tried a hot bed of coals covered with a few inches of dirt, but gave it up on finding that all too often they woke, suddenly and uncomfortable, at 2 A.M., in the middle of a spurious Indian fakir act but a decidedly genuine bed of red hot coals.

I slept with Tex and Al. Pooling our blankets, we attained a degree of softness and, Tex being rather chubby, a degree of warmth. The arrangement, however, was not entirely satisfactory. We took turns sleeping in the middle, which, though crowded (close, even) should have, it seemed to me, assured at least one of us of a good night's sleep. Tex and Al claimed otherwise; neither regarded me as a suitable bed-partner. "You . . . !" they said. "When you got the middle you wanna go to bed early. When you got the outside you wanna sit by the fire. You got such goddamn sharp elbows. When you're on the outside you roll up and take the blankets with you. (They fixed that, eventually, by spotting our bed near a large log and putting me next to the log.) When you're in the middle you curl up like a goddamn kitten."

(And *that* was a goddamn lie. With three in a bed the guy in the middle sleeps on his back, with his elbows close to his sides, and can't yawn until somebody gets out.) They said further that they pitied any woman I might ever marry and that I would never have a very successful married life anyway. As a matter of fact, they said, they only put up with me at all for the sake of our friendship. And because I happened to have a particularly warm and woolly blanket.

It was generally agreed, when our hike was over, that the only way to really sleep in the open is just to get completely exhausted.

When it was thought that individual soldiers were sufficiently trained to take care of themselves and their equipment, unit problems were instituted. Transportation being "authorized" on these occasions, we would load into our vehicles and roll through the countryside, eventually bivouac in what—it was hoped—was "our area," become "tactical," sit around for several days completely in the dark as to just what the hell was going on, learn one morning that we were no longer "tactical," and come back to camp.

These problems taught us that a battalion in the field is far from the compact unit that "dresses right" on a parade ground, whole companies having an ugly habit of becoming hopelessly lost, and large numbers of men, with vehicles, consistently taking the wrong turns. All this without the added confusion of the "roar of battle," the worst horror of war that we encountered being the perplexing directions given us by various civilians, all of whom insisted on refer-

ring to places as they were colloquially known rather than as they were marked on our maps. Outside of the general confusion our problems were chiefly notable for the utter lack of restraint shown by practically all of our drivers when confronted with long stretches of open road after weeks of driving on twisting tracks at a top speed of not more than fifteen miles per hour. Three that I knew, having the bad luck to meet (practically head-on) a brigadier general while travel-

ing at something considerably in excess of the recognized limit, were ignominiously deprived of their vehicles and reduced to Basic Privates, as of then. We learned to ride nonchalantly in the back of a peep, and decided that primarily our problems were not intended as training ventures at all, but were merely a means of impressing the civilian population with the wheeled might of the American forces overseas.

The population appeared suitably impressed, a great many
girls hanging far out of windows that they might wave at us,
and literally dozens of small children mobbing us for cigarettes were we foolish enough to stop.

Personally I was impressed not so much with the wheeled
might of the American forces as with the peculiarly tiny part
my life and limb and well-being played in the general
scheme of things. I realized—for the first time—that whole
companies, regiments even, could and would be serenely, if
not cheerfully, sent to slaughter did an occasion arise where
the "objective" was worth the casualties. And I was reminded of a phrase I'd read some place in an account of the
French-Indian Wars: So-and-so (a pretty rugged character,

I'd gathered) had come down the Hudson or up the Hudson or across the Hudson with "two hundred rifles." Well, here I was, a "rifle." Gas-operated, perhaps, instead of flintlock, but still a "rifle."

We learned to think accordingly. We grew contemptuous of the amenities and niceties of life; we developed an attitude that resembled not at all the Golden Rule; we learned to rely on and look after and out for ourselves—the hell with anybody else. We slept with our socks on. We got tough.

Our "staging area," it seemed, had been eminently successful.

WHILE THE RIGID TRAINING that we underwent in our staging area taught us, it was claimed, some very valuable things, our daily lives taught us at least as much. We lived in tents, in the woods. Of course, we couldn't say as much in our letters, nor could we send home any photos that might give an inkling of our whereabouts. In fact, several soldiers who tried to palm off some ancient prints taken during the Carolina Maneuvers were informed by the censors that such pictures couldn't be mailed under any circumstances. They had an "identifiable background." Thanks to this policy and (naturally) an enforced silence regarding our recent troop movement, families, mothers, wives, sweethearts, etc., "back in the States" thought we were still wherever it was we had been since first arriving in Australia. It was their idea that we still lived under tin; they saw pictures of Quonsett huts, and wrote us saying it was certainly nice we had clean cement floors underfoot.

Well, to begin with, our floors were sand—a peculiarly fine, dirty, dusty, gritty kind of sand that got in our beds and our shoes and our hair and our guns and took the enamel off Izzy Popopliss' false teeth. Later we got sawdust, and bit by bit, through a variety of nefarious schemes, most of us sooner or later acquired some kind of a real floor. Sergeant Rubitkish's tent (he happened to command a particularly sticky-fingered crew) managed to steal a large number of empty beer boxes which enabled them to floor their entire tent with boards that advertised, in big black letters, "XXXX Bulimba Beer." It made a very nice floor indeed, with a sort of linoleum effect. but sometimes when Sergeant Rubitkish's crew crawled out of bed following a night of inebriation and got smote in the face with dozens of big black XXXX Bulimba Beer's, they wished to God they'd stuck to sawdust.

When it got dark we went to bed. Later on candles were issued after a fashion, but we lowly privates saw very few of them. Spotlight, Nickel Plate, and the rest of the "Old Guard" cornered the candle market and used candles in a manner that led us to believe that they must certainly be eating them Eskimo style, or, at the very least, burning them at both ends. Eventually, of course, most of us obtained, in one way or another, some sort of a kerosene lamp. We relied on the government for our fuel, stealthily raiding the kitchen tank each night after dark, and thus, no doubt, adding considerably to the eventual cost of the war. But, we figured, what the hell? If we live through this trouble, we'll probably spend the rest of our lives paying for it, so let's get our share now. And if we didn't live—well, the eventual cost of the war would be no skin off our nose. George, g'wan up an' swipe some kerosene.

At first George, when swiping kerosene, invariably got himself lost on his way to the kitchen and wandered around in the dark for maybe an hour wailing, "Pe-e-e-ete! F' chrissake, where's the te-e-ent?" In addition to a great many trees, our woods was full of underbrush to the height of a man's shoulder. Soldiers getting up in the middle of the night spent as much as two hours looking for the latrine. Rather, the conscientious soldiers looked for two hours, there being some very strict rules against substituting anything, such as a large tree. Others settled for a fair-sized stump, "impersonated an officer," and went back to bed. Several soldiers who came in late during those first few weeks never did find their tents, but spent the night in the open, or—if they were lucky—found the latrine and waited there until a familiar face showed up. Often, as we sat huddled over a short stump of candle, a strange soldier would appear in the doorway and demand, "Where's Swede live?" Well, Swede didn't live within two hundred yards of us, but we always gave these strangers what help we could, pointing out in a vague sort of way the general direction they should take. We never convinced any of them. Usually they refused to admit that *they* were lost, but implied that it was Swede who was lost, or that we were deliberately trying to mislead them, and went off in a sulk and crashed around in the underbrush again. Some of them circled back to our tent (a moral victory for us); some just gave up, shrieked, "Oooooh, hell!" and struck off in what they hoped was the direction of their own tent. Some, no doubt, are still crashing around in the underbrush.

Eventually, of course, detail by detail, we hacked away a good share of the underbrush. This enabled us to see our next-door neighbors and learn that at some time in the not very immediate future our camp would be a very nice camp indeed, with mess halls, and water tanks, and even shower rooms. Several nondescript gangs, mostly composed of what appeared to be but partially reclaimed alcoholics, operating under the Allied Works Council (an organization that we insisted, not without foundation, was the "W.P.A. Overseas") showed up at highly irregular intervals, bummed us for cigarettes, and put in a few puttering hours on one of these installations. Which, frankly, rose no faster than had the pyramids.

In the meantime we ate picnic style, which may be jolly enough on the Fourth of July, but gets damn monotonous when carried to extremes. We learned to eat fast when the sun was out, before *all* the ants found us; and faster than hell when it was raining, it being very disconcerting to slup soup steadily for ten minutes, then look down and discover you still have just as much—if a somewhat thinner—soup as you ever had.

And until our shower room was ready for business (a day, incidentally, that we never saw) we hauled our water by truck, from large central tanks called the watering point. Delivered twice a day, in five-gallon cans, this water was supposed to be equally distributed between the kitchen and the wash rack, and *not* hauled off to individual tents. There was an unwritten law that urged that he who used the last of the water at the wash rack should go up to the kitchen and bring down another full can. This law was probably broken no more than the Volstead Act.

Not that it particularly mattered. Within a week every tent had a jealously guarded water can of its own, that was exchanged once a day—usually around ten o'clock at night—for one of the full cans left lying around the kitchen. Now and then some particularly ambitious private, on water detail for the day, would raid all the tents and steal everybody's water can. A commendable attitude, perhaps, but one that made him immediately and highly unpopular with all concerned. Originally too. there were some two dozen tin wash basins. supposedly part of the wash-rack equipment, and not to be removed under any circumstances. They did not long remain as anything that could be called public property. One by one they disappeared until there were only two left, both of which happened to be nailed to the rack. Presently they disappeared. This Army has no communistic spirit worth mentioning, but it can—and does—look after itself.

Some days, for one reason or another, we were short of water. Not to the point of suffering, perhaps, but short enough that four or even five men might find it necessary to wash in the same basin. Whether or not the fifth man in such cases emerged any cleaner for his efforts was highly debatable, but it was generally agreed that were the shortage acute enough the same water could be—and was—used as long as it would pour. Come to think of it, some of us who had favored numerous and prolonged baths in civilian life must have suffered at that; but most of us just dispensed with washing until our fingers stuck together.

We learned too, and quite rapidly, that a lot of other things that are supposed to drive those women who are described as being "good housekeepers" stark raving crazy, are just plain silly. I've got an Aunt who can't stand flies. If just one little fly gets inside Auntie's house she sounds a call to quarters, arms herself with flit and swatter, and goes after that fly, spraying and swatting indiscriminately.

Well, hell, Auntie. We lived (intimately) with a variety of creeping, crawling, flying, fluttering, slithering, burrowing, web-spinning things that hummed, buzzed, chirped, squeaked, croaked, droned, shrilled, and bit, stung, wounded, nibbled, annoyed, clung to, and walked over us. Through long familiarity my almost pathological fear of spiders dwindled to a mere distaste, and I flicked them away with my fingers as well as the next man. Anything, that is, up to the size of large tarantulas that looked not unlike the creations of some inexperienced but aspiring milliner. Having never seen any scorpions before, I didn't know enough to be afraid of them, but said, "Oh! Look at the little animals!" until somebody told me, "Jeezchrist! That's a *scorpion!*" and informed me it was better to kill them promptly with a large stick than admire them. All of us learned to shake our shoes before putting them on and dress in one minute flat.

If we took any longer the mosquitoes, trained to peel off at the same instant we did, droned down and went to work on those parts of the body that it is impossible to reach when you have your shirt over your head. Obviously they took us for punch boards and were all intensely interested in winning a kewpie doll. Naturally, we slept under nets, or "bars"

but the exact value of these contrivances was, we felt, open to debate. True, they kept a certain number of mosquitoes out; on the other hand, any mosquitoes that got inside, stayed inside. Some of us felt we would just as soon share the rest of Australia with several million mosquitoes as the inside of a net with two or three. When these pests became exceptionally bad (as they did, following so much as a heavy dew) I wore a head-net and fancied myself as resembling the approved version of a tropic adventurer. Some thought otherwise and called me "Grandma," but that was still better than slowly going punch-drunk from slapping the back of my neck.

Except for the bugs, the native wild life was anything but vicious. There were assorted lizards that looked horribly vicious, but evidently they had the same idea about us. Cornered, they would lash about rather ineffectually, like a Hollywood dinosaur, but given a choice they took off for the nearest tree and got up it as fast as they could, spiraling around and around so as always to be as far away from us as possible. At first we classed them with snakes and killed them on sight; later we ignored them. Now and then a kangaroo came hopping down the company street, hotly pursued by half a hundred yelling soldiers with some pretty far-fetched ideas about catching and eating this native Australian. There was another animal, a wallaby, we learned, that resembled a kangaroo built to scale and had the personality of an adventurous rabbit. They pattered into our tents quite regularly during the night time, and pattered out with anything edible they could carry. We thought this amusing rather than annoying and pretty well left them alone. There were possums and kookaburra birds. The latter looked like a crow in a dirty tux and had no manners to speak of, usually showing up in the nearest tree some forty-five minutes before Reveille and spoiling what would otherwise have been the

best part of a night's sleep with his raucous, rasping cawing. They were popularly known as "Laughing Jackasses" and unpopularly known by a variety of other blasphemous and biological names.

Every two or three days somebody with primeval instincts (or a particular liking for his last hour of sleep) would shoot one of these kookaburra birds, and the following day, at Retreat, we would listen to a short, pointed message concerning the advisability of "turning in all live ammunition immediately" and the dire and severe disciplining that would befall any man caught expending same in the future. We were given to understand that though he might be twelve thousand miles away, this was still the King's Forest, and poaching was strictly prohibited. Except, perhaps, with the bow and arrow, which, being noiseless, disturbed neither the King nor our colonel, a man who liked his little nap and didn't fancy a .30-.30 pouring through the side of his tent at odd moments.

However, we didn't try any archery. In fact, for all our simple, wholesome life, we didn't go native to any great extent, but remained quite civilized in most respects. A few took to wearing shorts that brought to light some extremely odd-looking legs and convinced us that the man who first introduced long trousers knew what he was about. On one other score we reverted to type. Almost to a man we grew or tried to grow a mustache, something that we had probably all longed to do back in civilian life, but hadn't had the necessary strength of spirit to try where there were people around—particularly young ladies—who might scoff at us. Army regulations state quite definitely that enlisted men will and must be "clean shaven" at all times, but we were a long ways from the War Department, and most of the C.O.'s concerned, probably in the interests of morale, allowed that at least a part of our faces might be something less. Consequently a truly amazing variety of hairy growths sprang up and were carefully nurtured. Most of them withered and died just previous to their owner's going on pass. Some went to seed, spread like ivy, and the C.O.'s—this time in the interests of sanitation—demanded that they come off. Some turned up missing following a particularly quick shave. I deliberately removed mine the day after somebody said, "Wipe the cocoa off'n your mouth."

Living as we did, so far from civilization, we grew to rely solely on the United States Army Service Forces for all our wants. And we found out what happened to the little boys who threw rocks at the blind newsboy—they'd grown up, joined the Army, and gone to work in the canteens. And now they had at their fingertips all the things we desired. Soap, shaving cream, razor blades, cigarettes, matches, Coca-Cola (whose reappearance convinced us the shipping situation was easier), everything that could possibly be classed as a luxury these thugs controlled. They were in a position to bully. And whether we liked it or them or not, we must needs be nice to them. So we were nice to them, friendly as all hell in fact, BUT WHEN THIS WAR IS OVER . . . As Sergeant Rubitkish put it: "Yu think those bastards was buyin' that stuff with their own money, an' tryin' to save everything they ever had."

Except for the personnel involved (and an overabundance of inventories), our canteens were a wonderful institution, taking the place of the Salvation Army, the Post Service Club, the local pub, and the still nonexistent U.S.O. They dispensed ice cream in three flavors and ice-cold Coca-Cola. Taking these ingredients back to our tents, we would mix them and drink "frosted cokes" while writing home describing our bare existence in the middle of the God-forsaken bush.

Beer, too, was G.I. Usually we received a ration of three bottles per man once a week, any known teetotalers being approached days in advance of "beer night" with wild offers of almost anything in any quantity would they only "lemme have your beer this week." We learned that beer can be appreciated and enjoyed without being served by a blond bar maid having a nice pair of legs.

Laundry, as always, was a bit of a problem. Sent out every other Tuesday, it came back—IF it came back—a week or so after all concerned had just about given up hope and opened a campaign with the supply sergeant for some new clothes.

When it did come, it came by the truckload and was dumped wholesale in the supply tent, where those who could convince anybody they'd sent laundry were allowed to paw through the mess until they found whatever it was they'd sent or a reasonable facsimile thereof. Naturally everybody went in with the idea that come what might *he* would "find" at least as many clothes as he'd sent away. Soldiers who were approximately the same size watched each other closely, suspiciously, like hawks, at all times; and it was sheer folly to reach for a size "30" anything while another size "30" was looking on.

When it came to amusing ourselves we had the usual games of chance, the regimental band, and movies. However, our company neither approved of nor appreciated the regimental band. This organization was quartered next to us and from very early in the morning until very late at night they practiced a variety of tunes on a variety of instruments, never more than four of them on the same tune, but all favoring heavy bass notes that made the trees quiver. They ate with us too, which made our chow line considerably longer, but were excused from furnishing any K.P.'s, another unending source of hate. We discussed all kinds of sabotage that we might wreak on our band. Particularly, we wanted to pour sand in the bass horn.

Sometimes, of course, the band did furnish us with a certain amount of entertainment. Otherwise we relied on our cinema, which, like the best in the States, had stars on the roof. As a matter of fact, the stars were the roof. Mostly the pictures themselves appeared to have been knocked out by Hollywood in something less than thirty-six hours for a cost of not more than seventy-five dollars including the premiere, but they were still movies. And we were still fans. Generally each picture was shown three nights running and we attended three nights running, until some of us who had also seen the same features a couple of times in civilian life could, with little or no effort, repeat all the punch lines from memory. Naturally enough, certain characters *did* repeat all the punch lines from memory, usually just prior to their appearing on the screen. We cheered madly when a familiar place or the old home state was mentioned. To a man, it seemed, we shrieked and whistled if a silk-clad feminine leg so much as flashed across the screen. We longed for those good old-fashioned newsreels full of sweepstakes winners and bathing beauties instead of London's latest blitz. We watched Travelogues of Tahiti and Havana ("The Pearl of the Caribbean")

and Tasmania and Old Mexico and wished that just once Mr. Fitzpatrick had gone to Kalamazoo.

All in all, we liked our "staging area" better than we had liked our "bloody resort plice," but we were still a long ways from home—a hell of a long ways from home—and overwhelmingly anxious and eager to see something, anything, that reminded us of the Main Streets we had known "back in the States."

YES, WE WERE A LONG ways from home. And just exactly what did we think about the whole business? Frankly, we didn't give the matter a hell of a lot of thought at any time. Arrangements that would make for warmer sleeping, future passes, the ever threatening Duty Roster, rumors, those and—the feminine companionship being what it was—fading mental pictures of a lot of girls in movie magazines; those were the things that filled our little minds.

Until, one morning, the newsboys who daily stormed our camp met us with late edition headlines that screamed: "JAPS THRU THE GAP—32 MILES FROM MORESBY."

We were alerted. They let the bars down. And when it has to, Brother, this Army can move. Willy-nilly we stripped off our denims, threw them in a truck that roared away, "To where they're dyeing them," somebody said. Not of a material that could be readily dipped or dyed ourselves (a fact, we agreed, that must surely have broken the Quartermaster's heart), we were presently issued half-pint bottles full of greenish fluid. "Skin dye," the guy said who was handing them out, and dashed off, his bare legs slapping through the brush. Ordered, "Give out these bottles" by a harried supply officer who was in no mood to be reasoned with, our hero hadn't had a chance to find any pants after removing his denims. He spent most of the day dashing thither and yon in a baggy pair of G.I. shorts.

We struck our tents, rolled our cots. Word got out that "You can take whatcha can carry on yu back." For the first time, our packs were too small. And suddenly we had too many clothes. A raincoat, a sweater, a field jacket, which to take? It never rains all the time—throw away the raincoat. A sweater? You won't need a sweater where you're going, Jack. A field jacket? Hell. Throw it away. And it was, literally, thrown away, wherever the owner happened to be when the idea struck him. Scattered heaps of every conceivable item: clothing, equipment, issue and otherwise, appeared where our tents had been. Shoes, shirts, garrison hats, two bicycles, a hand-powered sewing machine, magazines, souvenirs of Louisiana, Massachusetts, the West Coast and Australia, cards, shoe polish, old letters, shaving lotion, prized photos. The chips were down. Most of us took soap instead of the home-town sweetheart, and cigarettes had a priority on both.

But parting with some of our dearly beloved treasures was tougher than saying good-by the day we left for the induction center. I particularly noticed one Johnson, a stolid character, who had but recently, and at the expense of considerable effort, acquired a high-class kerosene lamp. For nearly twenty minutes, while the War Effort went on full blast all around him, Johnson sat mournfully on his cot, with three bars of P & G laundry soap in one hand, his wonderful lamp in the other. He fondled it, but unlike Aladdin, no good genii played Johnny-on-the-spot. Instead came Spotlight, roaring, "F'chrissake, Johnson, get your tail in gear!"

Johnson put his lamp on the ground. Somebody dropped a barracks bag on it. Our private lives, the backwash of War, lay splattered on the Company Street.

We ate presently, hurriedly and mostly out of cans, officers and men alike. The colonel's aluminum messware and an "E.M. Latrine" sign lay forgotten under the same broken table. Big Swede sliced great uneven chunks of bread, urged "Eat 'er oop, boys, this is the last time you'll ever see bread" in an accent as thick as his slices. Three of us grew practically poignant over a very ordinary can of apple butter labeled "Boise, Idaho. Made in the U.S.A." Home was all at once an awfully long ways away.

But—luckily and thank God—soldiers' minds are seldom emotionally channeled for more than three hours at a stretch. Either they get mad and blow their top, or they laugh it off. The horrible gone feeling that had come with our alert disappeared around two o'clock. We laughed it off. We almost enjoyed ourselves. Somebody opened their skin dye and wrote an obscene word on Wheel's back. It was thought a great gag by all who saw it.

When the Medics came around with iodine and sulfa pills, Old Pop, on the verge of realizing, at forty-one, a twenty-year urge to see "combat," asked a major to look at what he (Pop) thought was a very bad tooth. The major, assuming, no doubt, that he had personally discovered a potential deserter, peered suspiciously down Pop's throat, got met with a gummy expanse of nothingness. Pop had his teeth in his hand. Two PFC's snickered audibly, a first lieutenant coughed hurriedly, the major wrinkled his puss in what might well have passed for a smile.

Our denims came back, blotchy green, quite damp, and hopelessly muddled. The ensuing scramble made Macy's biggest bargain day look like a polite taffy pull.

When the boys from the Allied Works Council shuffled in for their daily puttering on what we thought might someday be our shower room and informed us that someday had practically arrived—that before the first of the month we would have showers—we could appreciate the irony of the situation. We made the usual vulgar remarks regarding what the AWC could do with their shower room.

It was a strain perhaps, but we could still laugh it off.

Church Services at 5 P.M. drew an even larger group than had attended while we were in convoy. An announcement to the effect that "last letters" could be turned in at the Orderly Room until 8 P.M. led to a flurry of writing. But there was too much to say that couldn't be said, and too many stomachs full of feelings that might be adequately presented were they branded on the stomach but shouldn't be attempted on paper. It would have been so very nice to tie up all the loose ends our lives had left us, but nobody would admit—least of all to himself—the need for such tying. Our letters, I'm afraid, were incoherent.

Supper consisted mostly of coffee.

Lined up at 8:30, our C.O. warned us of a split-second transportation schedule that would brook no lagging, questioned us concerning our water, rations, ammunition, and dog tags. His voice, in the darkness, sounded as if he were being strangled. Nickel Plate then called the roll. For one awful moment I thought: "I'll be damned if I answer!" But I did, in a voice that sounded strangely as if I were being strangled.

We loaded into trucks by the glare of headlights. A rasping voice, later identified as a Brigadier General, said quite distinctly, "The HELL with the speed limit! You get these men to Rauser [NOTE: Name is fictitious] Field in time for breakfast."

The ride to the field was, all in all, fairly miserable. Tex and Al and I sat huddled together (my turn in the middle) looking not at all like the three dashing musketeers of fiction. We talked a little, now and then, about nothing in particular. It was better than just sitting and much, much better than sitting and thinking. We slept some, between jolts. At one point, Tex and

Al both asleep, I amused myself with some morbid guesses on who, of the men in our truck, would be the first to "go." And I tried desperately to go back to sleep.

We arrived in time for breakfast—at 3 A.M. Like supper, it consisted mostly of coffee, though I very much doubt that any of us would have paid much heed had it been molten lava. We sloshed it down, stood around in the grayness while half a dozen transports waddled roaring to the ramp. In the east the first promise of a day spread up the sky; it looked about as promising as did our own futures at the time. The field lights blurred dimly through the ground mist.

As ordered we broke off in groups of thirty, trudged across the ramp, loaded into the bellies of the transports, deposited ourselves on the floor.

We took off.

There are no windows in transports. Probably it is just as well. But Sergeant Rubitkish, a man who would look on the bright side if his parachute failed, put it in words.

"I'm goddam glad," he said, "there wasn't nobody around to say g'bye to."